Religion in the
Contemporary South

Religion in the Contemporary South

Diversity, Community, and Identity

O. Kendall White Jr. and Daryl White, Editors

Southern Anthropological Society Proceedings, No. 28

Mary W. Helms, Series Editor

The University of Georgia Press

Athens and London

Southern Anthropological Society

Founded 1966

Published by the University of Georgia Press
Athens, Georgia 30602
© 1995 by Southern Anthropological Society
All rights reserved

Set in 11/13 Times
The paper in this book meets the guidelines for permanence and
durability of the Committee on Production Guidelines for Book
Longevity of the Council on Library Resources.

Printed in the United States of America

99 98 97 96 95   C   5   4   3   2   1
99 98 97 96 95   P   5   4   3   2   1

Library of Congress Cataloging in Publication Data
Religion in the contemporary South : diversity, community, and
    identity / O. Kendall White, Jr. and Daryl White, editors.
        p.   cm. — (Southern Anthropological Society proceedings ;
    no. 28)
    Includes bibliographical references.
    ISBN 0-8203-1675-X (alk. paper). — ISBN 0-8203-1676-8
(pbk. : alk. paper)
    1. Christianity—Southern States.   2. Southern States—Religion.
3. Religious pluralism—Southern States.   4. Religion and
sociology—Southern States.   I. White, O. Kendall.
II. White, Daryl.   III. Series.
GN2.S9243
[BR535 no. 28]
306.6'0975—dc20   94-9727

British Library Cataloging in Publication Data available

To Mary W. Helms
For her diligent and dedicated service
as Southern Anthropological Society Series editor

Contents

Religion in the
Contemporary South

Introduction

Daryl White and O. Kendall White Jr.

Writing almost three decades ago, Samuel Hill, the dean of southern religion scholars, argued that "no single feature" of the southern religious scene was "more revealing than the absence of pluralism and diversity from popular denominations" (1966:xvii). It was, in fact, its homogeneity that marked "Southern history as distinctive" and invited the crisis confronting the southern churches that he so perceptively analyzed. Nothing provided a better explanation for the South's persistent identity through the twentieth century as "the most conservative portion of the United States," according to Hill, than the "hold of orthodox Protestantism upon Southerners," even in face of "earth-shaking changes in industry, transportation, and education" (1988:12).

As we approach the end of the twentieth century, the orthodox Protestantism of which Hill spoke remains sufficiently entrenched among Southern Baptists, the nation's largest denomination, to survive intradenominational warfare, and to do so with even greater institutional hegemony (see Ammerman 1990 for an analysis of these conflicts). Indeed, acceleration of the social changes to which Hill alluded—industrialization, urbanization, and education, not to mention the emergence of high-tech industries and modern telecommunications—means that thousands of rural, southern immigrants to cities such as Atlanta, Dallas, Houston, Memphis, and Nashville must leave behind, as Robert Wuthnow observes, "an entire way of life" except for "the Baptist church" (1993:23–24). Not only does it remain a principal source of identity for those migrating to southern urban centers, but this southern brand of orthodox Protestantism is exported to northern cities through migration and telecommunications. In fact, Southern Baptist membership increased nationally by 32 percent between 1940 and 1985 (Finke and Stark 1992:248).

1

Wuthnow's intriguing analysis (1993) of American Christianity as it approaches the twenty-first century identifies the problems of materialism, religious diversity, and education as principal challenges for Christian denominations in their efforts to preserve religious communities and identities. Though his focus is Christianity, comparable challenges confront other religions in America. In fact, it may be argued that the political-historical development of American society established a social order and cultural milieu in which all religious movements face essentially the same fundamental problems (White 1972; Herberg 1960).[1] Thus, Will Herberg, in his classic book *Protestant, Catholic, Jew* (1960), argued that these religions succeeded not by maintaining their distinctiveness but through embracing a "religion of the American way of life" and conferring a form of identity on immigrants that was compatible with their American experience. Immigrants could demonstrate just how American they were by their identification with and participation in their respective religious communities. In short, Herberg's analysis explained how American society could build a common cultural base out of its religious pluralism.

Hill (1966:40–50) argues that Herberg's thesis is not applicable to the South. Since the latter did not experience patterns of foreign immigration similar to those of other regions, it was characterized less by religious pluralism than by religious hegemony. No region in the country, with the possible exception of the Rocky Mountains by the Mormons, was more dominated by nor more defined in terms of religion. Traditional southern identity is inextricably linked with southern Protestantism (see also Hill 1972:24–56). As rebellious as the South may often appear, however, no region seems more preoccupied with proclaiming its patriotism and "Americanism" nor with identifying religion with culture. The South takes a back seat to none in linking religion to the "American way of life" and appropriating its identity through religious, national symbols. In this sense, Hill is wrong. Celebrated in terms of the gospel of America, the religious identity embodied in traditional southern Protestantism may not have required the reconciliation with religious pluralism occurring elsewhere, but religious identity became as significant, if not more so, regionally and personally in the South than elsewhere in America. Moreover, it assumed the role posited by Herberg as the symbolic link to national identity.

From a contemporary vantage point, the problem may be conceptualized differently. Given the hegemony of white southern Protestantism, the South may not have required something comparable to the religious identity of which Herberg speaks to have integrated diverse elements (immigrants and religious pluralism) into a whole (the "American way of life"). The southern identification of religion with nationalism functioned more as an attempt to legitimate southern claims vis-à-vis those of the nation than as a mechanism of social integration. Those aspects of Herberg's analysis that were dependent on immigration and religious pluralism are, however, much more pronounced in the South today. Like the nation, the South now confronts problems of religious diversity, maintaining community, and preserving religious and regional identities as we move into the twenty-first century. Thus the polarities identified by Wuthnow (1993:13–14)—diversity vs. uniformity, community vs. individualism, liberalism vs. conservatism, and public vs. private—as paradigms for anticipating the future of American Christianity portend much the same for religion in a South that is more diverse and less unlike the nation than when the analyses of Herberg and Hill first appeared.

METHODOLOGY

The significance of community and identity are especially responsive to the traditional ethnographic research of anthropologists. Employing direct and participant observation techniques, in which it is possible to examine the rituals and behavior of those among whom they labor, several of these scholars provide us with insight into popular religious phenomena. Through participant observation, Valerie Fennell, for instance, identifies subtle changes in the relative power of men and women and documents a pervasive tendency toward the feminization of religion in her study of gender relations in fourteen local congregations, thirteen Protestant and one Catholic, in a small southern town. And Mary Anglin, again as a participant observer at the congregational level, demonstrates how working-class Christian Fundamentalists empowered themselves in their struggle with mine owners through appeals to the Bible and support from the congregation. From Melinda Wagner's observation of classes in Christian Fundamentalist schools, it is evident that they share more in common with their secular counterparts than the "total institutions" with which they are typically identified. Participating in the congregational life and other religious activities of the

Temple of Spiritual Truth, a pseudonym for an African American Spiritual storefront church in Nashville, Hans Baer describes this religious community's endowment of its members with a sense of power and dignity missing in their secular lives. And Sharlotte Neely's twenty-year ethnographic research among the Snowbird Cherokee demonstrates how Christianity provides a unique basis for preserving Cherokee identity. It is their potential for identifying subtleties of social phenomena that render these direct and participant observation techniques of ethnographic research so useful.

Some of the research in this volume reflects the current trend toward the turning inward of the anthropologist's gaze to analyze her or his own experience and culture. Though sometimes criticized for its lack of objectivity (see Knowlton 1992), at its best "native anthropology" produces a reflective "withinness" enabling a scholar to apply the analytical models of the discipline to meanings enjoyed as a native participant. Faye Harrison's family reunion constituted a religious pilgrimage integrating the Harper family with ancestors and extended kin through the celebration of emancipation rituals and a religious family culture recalling members to reproduce politically informed behavior in their own lives; Brenda Stewart's experience as a Unitarian Universalist enables her to appreciate this community's delineation of boundaries between itself and southern Christianity in the social construction of its alien identity; Miles Richardson analyzes ritual aspects of speaking and hearing as means of apprehending the sacred in his native Southern Baptist tradition, a clear contrast with the touching and seeing characteristic of liturgical traditions such as Catholicism. These three examples of native anthropology illustrate its capacity to uncover deeper levels of meaning by applying anthropological tools to familiar experience.

Other researchers relied on historical materials and literary documents for their data. Though not traditionally identified with anthropological methodology, anthropologists often shed new light on historical phenomena through the distinctive preoccupations of the discipline and the use of anthropological theory as interpretive schemata. Thus, McDonogh examines the role of anti-Catholicism, historically identified with southern Protestantism, in the shaping of identity for southern Catholics. The pervasive conception of southern Protestants as intolerant fundamentalists, which owes much to the debate over biological evolution, was largely created and is currently perpetuated by secularists whose writings provide the data for Smout's analysis, "Attacking (Southern) Creationists." Most of the scholars writing for this volume have not relied on a singular methodological technique but were more eclectic as they employed research strategies most consistent with understanding the phenomenon under investigation as well as adjusting to contingencies of the research process.

DIVERSITY, COMMUNITY, AND IDENTITY

Though the Southern Baptists remain the dominant religious body in the South and continue to define the tenor of much of the region's culture, the issues of multiculturalism and religious pluralism that grip the rest of the nation resonate in today's South. With our neglect of Judaism, Islam, Buddhism, mainline Protestant denominations, Mormonism, and some of the new religions, this volume underreports the South's religious diversity while emphasizing the significance of the challenges to community and identity that Wuthnow (1993) identifies with contemporary American Christianity. His argument that religious identity is defined and preserved through denominations, "communities of memory," and communities of support applies equally to the southern experience. The following essays examine the role of ritual in the creation and preservation of religious community and identity, processes of boundary delineation in which religious identities are negotiated through imposition and choice, the community as social control and support in constructing religious identities, and the integration of religious and regional identity.

The essays by Miles Richardson, Jon Anderson and Gwen Kennedy Neville, Faye Harrison, and Sharlotte Neely illustrate how ritual symbolically links individuals to a tradition and past. While speech and writing, conversation and text provide the crucial information and knowledge, ritual revitalizes cultural traditions, connecting participants in the present and the past, through the social construction of a community of memory. Thus, Richardson's analysis of the Southern Baptist sermon as a "speech event," which establishes the centrality of speaking and hearing as modes of apprehending the sacred among Southern Baptists, demonstrates that they construct and preserve their religious community and identity through ritual processes no less than liturgical traditions that rely more heavily on touching and seeing as avenues to the holy.

For Catholics in the South, the ritualization of time, with both a general church calendar and a more specific southern congregational one, which Anderson and Neville describe, shows how Catholics have constructed a community of memory that both delineates boundaries between themselves and other southerners and links them to their southern neighbors. With their integration into a worldwide institution stretching back centuries, southern Catholics enjoy a transcendent identity separating them from the South by particularizing and minimizing the American southern experience while their congregational time, which is more consistent with the typical southern Protestant calendar, integrates them into their local communities and affirms their regional identity. The Harper family reunion, analyzed by Faye Harrison, provides a ceremonial coming together of descendants of a former slave family. Not only are kinship and ecclesia integrated through religious rituals, but the community of memory is preserved by recounting the sacrifices and retelling the stories of courageous forebears who endured slavery, celebrated emancipation, struggled through segregation, and participated in the civil rights movement. Having ritualized and preserved the past, the family reunion becomes a call to responsible citizenship—to political and religious consciousness and action—empowering African Americans and preserving the Harper family. Sharlotte Neely describes the "Trail of Tears Singing" organized and sponsored by the Zion Hill Baptist Church of the Snowbird Cherokees that brings together the Cherokee Nation along with many local and out-of-state whites. Rekindling the memory of the historic Trail of Tears, with sixteen thousand Cherokees forcibly relocated and at least four thousand fatalities, this modern "singing" reinforces the identity of today's Cherokees as a Native American ethnic group still confronting dilemmas of acculturation.

The conflict between conferred and chosen identities appears in the analyses of Kary Smout, Gary McDonogh, and Brenda Stewart. Though Smout provides us with no information about the identities creationists assume for themselves, he discusses the rhetorical techniques employed by secularists to discredit creationists by identifying them with a naive southern Fundamentalism labeled as backward and ignorant—an imposed identity apparently enjoying considerable popular support both inside and outside the South. The portrayal of Catholics as a threat to southern culture and the Pope as the anti-Christ that appears among southern Protestants has profoundly shaped the identity of Catholics in the American South. As McDonogh amply documents, this nativism made it difficult for white southern Catholics to feel comfortable in the South though they participated in the regional racism that perpetuated a boundary between black and white Catholics. Brenda Stewart finds many Unitarian Universalists rejecting an identity as Christian, a phenomenon probably most pronounced in the South because of southern Protestantism's peculiar appropriation of the label of Christian. Consciously choosing to define themselves as "alien" to popular southern culture, Unitarian Universalists are a growing segment of the new religious culture of the South. These three cases—creationists, southern Catholics, and Unitarian Universalists—present us with conferred or chosen identities whose meanings are derived from social conflict with an Other presented as an oppositional or negative identity.

Confronting dominant cultural forces construed as hostile may lead to the development of separate institutions for boundary delineation. Melinda Wagner's research on fundamentalist schools provides a fascinating example of consequences of the social and cultural changes at work in the contemporary South. The apparent irony in the need for a regionally dominant fundamentalist tradition to establish its own educational institutions illustrates how dominant cultural forces have made the South more like the nation, underscoring the breakdown of southern Protestantism's hegemony. Even so, Wagner does not find in the typical fundamentalist school a total institution sharply delineating cultural boundaries. On the contrary, she observes a process of cultural accommodation in which much of the secular agenda characterizing public schools, including pedagogical techniques, is incorporated into an institution consciously defined by conservative religious values. The traditional values of biblically oriented southern fundamentalists, with their local churches providing a community of support, empowered the workers observed by Mary Anglin in their confrontation with mine owners. Using the Bible as the basis for ideological support, these fundamentalist Christians found religious grounds for their civil disobedience and deconstruction of the privileged claims of mine owners.

The four essays focusing on African American religion underscore the significance of community structure and support for the sustenance of identity. While Harrison's analysis of the Harper family reunion shows how this celebration preserves a community of memory, as previously noted, Hans Baer's study of a Spiritual congregation in Nashville

demonstrates how the social structure of the congregation, with its development of titles and offices, provides a sense of dignity and identity
that is often denied to these believers in their experience with institutions dominated by whites. The significance of continuity and change
appears in the ethnography by Mona Phillips, Andrew Billingsley, and
Fleda Jackson of an Atlanta congregation in which contemporary Afrocentric and traditional Baptist qualities are combined. While the necessity of change is clearly embodied in an elderly sister's proclamation that
"the wind blows, so why not change?," the respect for tradition appears
in the pastor's pronouncement that "there are some things you leave
alone. The Nurses Guild you don't bother." As an African religion, the
Yoruba communities in South Carolina and in Atlanta, Georgia, enjoy
much of their appeal from the use of southern experience in the forging
for black men of alternative identities to those traditionally imposed by
the region. Beatriz Morales describes the experience of Baba Kunle,
who consciously chose to establish his community in the South, both redefining racial meanings and enhancing the integration of racial, ethnic,
religious, and regional identities.

In the works by Michael Angrosino, Valerie Fennell, and Scott
Thumma, we see still more emphasis on the interconnections of regional
and religious identities. The Indo-Americans in Tampa, Florida, whom
Angrosino studied, come from Hindu backgrounds but religiously be-
have more like typical middle-class Americans. Instead of emphasizing
traditional forms of private meditation or spiritual development, they
use church involvement to promote civic virtues. Thus the diversity of
Hinduism is homogenized into a single amalgam—a sort of nondenominational or ecumenical blend—expressed largely in English, enabling
the Indo-American community to establish religious and civic organizations to promote religious pluralism, multiculturalism, educational
reform, and various civic policies. Valerie Fennell's research on the
fourteen congregations of Curlew Point finds them organized in terms of
traditional southern values regarding race and gender, with nine Euro-
American congregations, four African American, and only one racially
mixed. While women did most of the work to maintain vital religious
congregations, the official ritual and ceremonial roles of religion and the
formal offices were occupied by men, which, Fennell argues, preserves
the distinction between the power of men and women in public and private spheres. Her conclusions are consistent with those historians who

identify a long-term trend toward the feminization of religion in American society. Finally, Thumma's examination of a racially mixed, mega congregation in Atlanta, Georgia, clearly identifies the techniques used to forge a collective identity that corresponds to the emergent image of Atlanta as the cosmopolitan embodiment of the contemporary South. Employing the image of the phoenix rising out of the ashes with the backdrop of the Atlanta skyline, the church portrays itself as a racially integrated fulfillment of Martin Luther King Jr.'s dream.

Samuel Hill may be correct when he argues that the functions of the religious celebration of the American way of life that Herberg identified with Protestantism, Catholicism, and Judaism were not applicable to the South. Since the region experienced less immigration and was religiously homogeneous, a mechanism for assimilating immigrants and accommodating religious pluralism was hardly necessary. However, the South today is more like the nation. With profound economic changes, increased immigration and urbanization, and greater religious diversity, today's South confronts problems of social integration similar to those analyzed by Herberg. The essays in this volume, with their focus on religious community and identity, examine movements and organizations that are wrestling with problems of religious and ethnic diversity, sometimes preserving or forging a regional, southern identity. In their documentation of a vibrant religiosity, at the very least these essays underscore the persistence of religion in the face of modernity and raise a central question that follows from Durkheim's legacy. Can religion be a principal source of social integration in a modern, even postmodern, society characterized by multiculturalism and religious pluralism? Today, this question is no less relevant for the South than for the nation.

NOTE

1. Like the current implications of multiculturalism, religious pluralism historically posed problems of social integration for American society. Social integration was realized, according to Herberg (1960), as Protestantism, Catholicism, and Judaism adapted to American society as three branches of a religion of the American way of life. Identifying with one of these religions, immigrants could affirm their Americanness without having to abandon their particular religion. Robert Bellah (1967) describes the evolution of a more

dynamic and transcendent civil religion, in which the Judeo-Christian tradition provides symbols and myths for the sacralization of American experience, which enhanced societal integration while facilitating religious pluralism. He finds Americans typically embracing two religions, a shared civil religion and a personal or denominational one. While the latter produces separate communities, the former integrates these into the social fabric. White (1972) presents an alternative explanation for the social integration of religious pluralism in America through political, not religious, culture. The emergence of constituting norms defining appropriate organizational structure and interorganizational relations for religious groups compelled the latter to accept the legitimacy of religious pluralism and to subordinate certain interests to the state if they were to function successfully within the society. In this account, social integration is achieved less through the active role of religion than by religious adaptation to political culture.

Part 1

Ritual and a Community of Memory

Speaking and Hearing (in Contrast to Touching and Seeing) the Sacred

Miles Richardson

We humans, we primates, sibling to the chimpanzee, cousin to the gorilla, true members of the mammalian family, nonetheless speak. The world in which we *live* is that of a sexually dimorphic, warm-blooded, bipedal vertebrate; the world in which we *are* is that of the multivocalic, transcendent symbol. We are simultaneously creatures of the mouth and people of the word. Precariously situated between gene and phonemic, we forever crisscross boundaries, asserting the determinism of chemistry and the freedom of poetry, only to reverse this assertion with the proposition that the hand speaks while the word caresses.

Religion, seemingly so transcendent an endeavor, achieves physical strength through a manipulation of the primate sense modalities of sight, touch, smell, taste, and sound. Drawing on Rappaport (1971), we may suggest that the manipulation of the sense modalities in the name of the holy constitutes ritual. Ritual, which so closely resembles the epigamic displays of other animals, paradoxically allows us to communicate to one another the sense of the sacred, or that which is ineffable. That which is ineffable is literally that which cannot be spoken. We manipulate primate modalities in the name of the holy to communicate that which we cannot name. Truly paradoxical creatures, we humans!

In the quest to communicate the holy, the different senses, overlapping though they are, nonetheless lend themselves to an array of different emphases. Sight, the distancing sense, establishes an external presence, a scene that lies ahead and beyond ourselves. Touch also shows that objects are out there; in so doing, however, touch may also permit us to separate the subjective self who lies within from the objective presence that resides without. Smell and taste are proximate senses, and

taste is as tactile as touch. But in a manner much more direct than any of
the other senses, taste, through the mouth, brings the outside world inside and thereby transforms the external into us. Sounds, ejected by the
mouth and received by the ear, are closer than visions and reverberate
within. Similarly, while sight allows us to privately scrutinize a person's
face and examine it for clues, sound requires us to ask again for what
we miss; consequently, sight, being silent, is more contemplative, while
sound, being noisy, is more social (Ong 1969).

Within the single religion of Christianity, we find a continuum of emphases. At the liturgical end of the spectrum, visual sacraments create a
sense of an objective awe to the contemplative viewer; at the evangelical
end, sounds produce subjective conviction among the congregational
participants:

At the altar, the hands of the priest lift the wafer of unleavened bread,
which becomes now, at this sacrificial moment, before the kneeled
parishioners, the body of Christ.

"Somebody touched me," the lead tenor of the gospel quartet sings
in Pentecostal fervor, to which the quartet replies, "It must have been
the hand of the Lord." [1]

Baptists of the American South, particularly those belonging to
churches affiliated with the Southern Baptist Convention, follow the
tenor's lead.

Having stripped the meeting place of all statues and crucifixes, having
renounced all sacraments and having introduced ordinances whose message is "purely symbolic and free of magic," and having secularized
their meetings and having reduced the hand to a metaphor, the Baptists
opt for the word (Richardson 1990). Everywhere the Bible, the Holy
Word of God, inerrant to many, infallible to most, and sufficient to all
(Patterson 1971), proclaims its importance. On the sign in the front
lawn, beneath the name of the church, "For God so loved the world. . . .
John 3:16"; above the entrance door, ". . . let us go into the House
of the Lord. Psalm 122:1"; and above the baptistery, where the former
sinner is immersed to be reborn in Christ, "This is my beloved son. . . .
Matthew 3:17"; the Bible is quoted, chapter and verse. Their own personal copies of the Book of Books clasped in their hands, people enter
the church from Bible study, with the sounds of the Sunday school nurs-
ery song fresh in their remembrance, "Yes, Jesus loves me. The Bible

tells me so." In the pews, extra copies of the Bible await alongside the Baptist hymnal; on the huge table beneath the pulpit, the table for the Lord's Supper, which bears the inscription from Luke 22:19, "This Do in Remembrance of Me," rests a large, open Bible; and on the massive pulpit, the preacher places his own much-used volume, which, at the beginning of his sermon, he opens with an invitation to the congregation, "Please turn with me to Galatians, chapter 2, verse 20, 'I am crucified,' Paul said in his letter to the Galatians, 'I am crucified with Christ; nevertheless I live; yet not I, but Christ liveth in me.' "

People whose speaking I am speaking about are those who call themselves Southern Baptists, and in their calling, region and faith, southern and Baptist, tend to merge into one. Historically, the destiny of the two are intertwined. The Baptists of the South broke with the Baptists in the north over the issue of slavery to form the Southern Baptist Convention, and following the Civil War, they displaced the Methodists as the principal Protestant church. Today, they have become the country's largest Protestant denomination, and although having expanded far beyond the South, they cling tenaciously to the regional identification and to a broadly conservative, if not fundamentalist, agenda. They also remain largely white (Rosenberg 1989).

To speak about speaking obviously calls for an approach centered in discourse (Sherzer 1987). Broadly stated, a discourse-centered approach describes how we in the ongoing present shape the living experience of a bipedal primate into the symbol world in which we are. As Urban and Sherzer indicate (1988), such an approach focuses on language as used. In the construction of their Christworld, that part of their symbolic reality central to their identity, the Southern Baptists use language both in the oral and written forms. To the ethnography of speaking, we must add the ethnography of reading. We must also consider the extra-linguistic context in which discourse occurs; speaking and reading do not transpire between brain cells but are placed by a material setting into particular situations (Richardson and Dunton 1989). These two considerations, language in use and the material setting, allow us to describe, at least, how discourse constitutes culture. Thus, a discourse-centered approach attends to the ongoing now, to the present instances of concrete accusations between flesh-and-blood people as to the significance of their lives. In the construction of their Christworld,

Southern Baptists draw on the past, but even when addressing the past, which they do every Sunday, they constitute the present, for, to quote the preacher quoting the Apostle Paul's letter, "Christ liveth in me."

And Christ liveth in the Word. We must position the Southern Baptist biblical usage within the range of Christianity, which, after all, perhaps by as early as the first century A.D., became a religion of the Book, of written speech and narrative discourse. On the liturgical, object end of the spectrum, reading the Bible is an essential part of the Catholic mass, yet even after Vatican II, the sacrificial offering of Christ's body and blood present in the wafer and the wine in the priest's hands transforms secular actions into sacred ritual. Seeing and touching are the principal religious modalities. On the radical, subject end, Pentecostals likewise read the Sacred Word, but it is the moment when the Holy Spirit descends on them that transforms ordinary speech into sacred tongues. Speaking and hearing the sacred are their primary experiential forms. More radical than liturgical, Southern Baptists also "open up their hearts for that still, quiet voice" and seek "to talk to God through prayer," but the authoritative path to the divine is the Bible; it is for them, as for other Christian, "high church" conservatives, their liturgical object.

The Bible is authoritative, because, according to the statement accepted by the Southern Baptist Convention, "It has God for its author, salvation for its end, and truth, without any mixture of error, for its matter" (Patterson 1971:1590). For the fundamentalist, the Bible is inerrant, that is, being divinely inspired (2 Timothy 3:16) the Bible is without error (Geisler 1980); for the conservative, the Bible is infallible, that is, the Bible is not fallible in accomplishing its purpose to reveal God to humans (Barnhart 1986). Consequently, for both positions, fundamentalist and conservative, and perhaps even for the moderates among the Southern Baptists, the Bible is God speaking. It is not simply a source of information, but the very voice of God (Packer 1980).

The Bible as text, thus, claims special status in the hierarchy of texts. The fixity of text that Ricoeur (1979) notes as characteristic of written discourse is squared by the doctrines of inerrancy and infallibility. Such fixity poses a special challenge to the phenomenological or constructionist's view of reading, in which the act of reading constitutes the text (Suleiman 1980). As part of the doctrine of the priesthood of believers, the Baptist view of reading is that the Bible is available to all. God speaks plainly, so any reader, no matter how unschooled that person may be, can read God's Word (Marsden 1980).

We can, however, distinguish at least two reading acts: (1) those occurring in the various Baptist seminaries in which scholars, schooled in Greek and Hebrew, argue which interpretation most closely approximates the original written texts, the Autographia, which all agree do not exist; and (2) the reading occurring in a worshipping context.

In a worshipping context, an individual, the epitome of the solitary reader, alone with a text, may read the Bible at home, perhaps as part of a private desire to read the book from cover to cover. Individual readings, however, often become part of public readings. Much of Sunday school is devoted to people reading to each other. On occasions, people quote biblical passages, and here reading moves toward speaking. The most public of all readings is when the preacher, as he takes to the pulpit to deliver his sermon, reads to the seated congregation the text he has chosen for his sermon. This reading, depending on the mood the preacher intends to set, may be quiet and thoughtful or much more dramatic, with interjections for the congregation to listen well "to what the Lord saith." While many in the congregation may content themselves with a listening, others turn to the passage and read silently along with the preacher's reading. Once the initial reading is accomplished, the preacher moves from reading to speaking, but during the course of the speaking he may return to the Bible on his pulpit, take it in his hand, display it before the congregation's eyes, and read again the same passage or a closely related one to add the ring of conviction to his sermon. Reading, then, even here, or perhaps especially here in the inerrancy of text, has an authority, bolstered by the visual display, that speaking lacks.

Speaking, on the other hand, has the immediacy, the lived-in-present quality that reading as reading destroys (Chafe and Tannen 1987). Baptists come to church on Sunday to hear the Word of God preached, that is, spoken.

The preached Word of God, the sermon, is the principal form of verbal communication in which the Christworld comes to be among the Baptists. It occupies a particular time and place, chronologically, spatially, and linguistically. Chronologically, it appears on Sunday, principally in the morning but also again at night. Spatially, it occurs in that part of the church structure formerly called the auditorium, but now increasingly, as Baptists go upscale, the sanctuary. Linguistically, it occupies the final half of a range of discourse, labeled the Sunday Morning Worship Service.

As we enter the foyer, the attendant hands us a printed program, from which we read the sequence of who will deliver what. As the hour approaches, the music director, who orchestrates the first half of the service, welcomes us and asks that we turn to "Hymn number 181, 'Wonderful Words of Life.' 'Sweetly echo the gospel call; offer pardon and peace to all.' All together now. . . ." From that song, the director moves us to additional songs, through the announcements, and into prayers offered by a respected male member of the congregation, and finally to a solo performance by a choir member, often a woman. During the silence following the solo, the preacher, seated on the platform beneath the choir, rises, walks to the giant pulpit centered in front of the congregation, and begins.

The sermon, always based, however loosely, on a reading of the Bible, Old Testament or New, moves from the reading of the printed word to direct delivery of the spoken. The sermon is not a religious ritual in the sense that the Catholic mass is, which, as a performance, reenacts the sacrifice of Christ and whose theological efficacy is independent of the parishioner's beliefs or even attention. In contrast, for the sermon to be efficacious, there has to be an audience, however inattentive.

The audience is the congregation of a particular church, which, in Baptist terms, is a band of baptized believers, a voluntary association based not on residence in a particular location but on a public proclamation of the individual's belief in Jesus Christ as Savior and public immersion in the church's baptistery. Experientially, the congregation in Erving Goffman's terms (1961; 1981) is a focused gathering, a group whose being alternately coagulates and dissolves, not unlike attendance at a lecture. The lecturelike quality is augmented by the absence of religious icons and the presence of a speaker on a raised platform with a podium speaking to a seated audience. Yet, the sermon, while it may include the lecturelike qualities of a speaker gazing out and an audience looking up, is clearly not a lecture, because no Baptist goes to church to hear a sermon read.

Baptist sermons, in the words of one Baptist commentator, are more doctrinal than theological, more affirmative than explanatory, more hortatory than logical, and finally more oral than literary (Allen 1958). To the anthropological listener, the Baptist sermon is, first and foremost, a speech event.

A sermon has a number of discourse features that various preachers use. Immediacy, however, is the common goal of these features. The doctrine of inerrancy promotes a reading of the text that is not necessarily one of probing, dismantling, pondering, restoring, the type of reading that accompanies a more broadly interpretive essay into the text. Reading is more inductive, a searching through God's storehouse of facts, to discover what the Bible says. What the Bible says is the Word of God, and the purpose of preaching is to interpret the Sacred Scripture, which means speaking the Gospel. Preaching aims to make an eternal text live in the present, in the momentary blinking of the now.

Speaking the Gospel is presenting God's storehouse of eternal truths in the language of the people. Yet the sermon draws on the language of the Scripture for its rhetoric. In the past, this rhetoric has leaned heavily on the English of the King James translation of the Bible: "And he sware unto her, Whatsoever thou shall ask of me, I will give it thee, unto the half of my kingdom" (Mark 6:23). Quoting the King James English, an English long-since departed from standard discourse, helps mark what the preacher speaks as sermonic. Although other, more modern translations of the Sacred Scriptures find their way into Baptist discourse, the King James Bible remains the sentimental, if not the preferred, version for preachers and their congregations.

To make the text live now, the preacher must live. He, and in member churches of the Southern Baptist Convention 99.99 percent of the preachers are men, must convince the congregation that he speaks as one called by God. Preachers commonly report two great events in their lives, both more important than their marriage. The first is their conversion from being lost to being saved, and the second, which often is reported to come unannounced and unsought for and, indeed, initially to be resisted, is the call to preach. The call to preach is a verbal command from God. Rarely does the preacher report that he saw God; never, as far as I know, does he report an external vision in the manner of a Spanish American Catholic who, in the traditional accounts, might see Christ's image on a rock or find an image of the Virgin by a stream. The call to preach sets the preacher apart from the rest of us, for through him God speaks. While the sermon begins with a reading, speaking by a man moved by God soon takes charge.

Traditionally, the necessity of speaking God's Word has meant a disdain for the carefully crafted sermon. " 'Schoolin' ain't necessary as long as I've got good wind' " (Dale 1958), the reputed motto of the early backwoods preacher, still resonates within the more learned discourses of the day. How can one speak the inspired words of God if one devotes all that attention to searching the dictionary for an elegant phrase? Form, written form, stands in opposition to sincerity. Today, even in upscale churches, with cushioned pews and stereophonic choirs, preachers, when they want to show they are truly inspired, cast aside the prepared text and revert to southern vernacular. "Poor old Samson, now, he had a girl problem" (heard at Istrouma Baptist Church in 1985; see note 1). "Give is a Christian word. Getting, on the other hand, to be getting all the time is like being an animal, like a hog with all four feet in the trough" (heard at University Baptist Church in 1981). "Back in the thirties, grocery stores had a charge list. You paid up every week. You paid and your debt was canceled. Now, you had to make sure it was, or that debt might still be there next week. Christ's death cancels our debts. His blood washes it away, so clean even the sign of it is gone" (heard at Jefferson Baptist Church in 1981).

Narratives are another device for making the text live. The narrative of conversion is a common genre (Harding 1987; Stromberg 1990). Baptists believe, as do most Christians, that they are born in sin. They do not, however, believe in infant baptism. Instead, they hold that a person must reach the age of reason before that person can realize the magnitude of personal sin and fully commit herself or himself to Jesus. Thus, when the preacher speaks of the conversion experience of a famous individual, or when he, at a time when the need is great, speaks of his own awakening, he recaptures, reembellishes, retells in speech form, the principal moment in a Baptist life, and in the retelling, reestablishes that experience in each life of those in the congregation.

Narratives of Jesus' day are another strategy for vivifying the eternal text. Depending on the inclination of the preacher, these narratives may include comments about customs at the time of Jesus, wrapping babies in swaddling clothes, for example, or about geography ("Now just where is the Sea of Galilee?"), or about events in Jesus' life, such as when he cast out the money changers from the temple. The narratives close the gap between the ongoing now, the time of the late twentieth century, and the days of Jesus. To narrow the gaps, the narratives commonly include reported speech: "Now when Jesus, there on the cross, turn his head skyward and said, 'My God, my God, why hast thou forsaken me?' what did he mean?"

If the Bible in general is inerrant and divinely inspired, how much more precious are the actual words of Jesus? So precious in fact that they appear in red in special editions of the King James text, red as "the precious blood of the Lamb" himself. In reporting the sacrificial speech of Jesus, the preacher, when speaking to the congregation, seeks, always, to establish the reality of Christ's sacrifice, by restoring an oral presence to the eternal text. Reported speech allows the speaker to combine authority, the authoritative voice of Jesus' words, stained in red, with his own voice, one called by God, to speak the sacred.

We know Jesus' life through texts. These texts presumably were written sometime later than the life they report, and again presumably, they report what already was talked about, that is, the life of Jesus existed as oral telling before it became written (Kelber 1983).[2] So in speaking the words that the text said Jesus spoke, the preacher circumvents time and returns to the primitive church, the church before it became liturgical. For Southern Baptists, this short circuiting has particular significance. In the Baptist theory of Christian succession, held implicitly by many and argued vehemently by some, Baptists are not and have never been Protestants. Throughout history, the false church, that is, the Roman Catholic church and all its offspring, and the true church, the Baptist, have existed along side, with the Roman Pope persecuting and the Baptists being persecuted. Officially, the Southern Baptist Convention does not accept this theory of succession, but individual Southern Baptists remain convinced that their own congregation, as a band of baptized believers, is the true, spiritual, if not lineal, descendant of the Jerusalem church (Wamble 1964; Shurden 1972).

Eventually, usually at the stroke of twelve noon on Sunday, the sermon ends. The preacher has recited the last verse, has told his final story, and now turns to the closing speech event, the Invitation. This is "the last opportunity you might have, the last chance to turn your life around, to turn it over to Jesus. Now, while the choir sings the invitational hymn, 'Only Trust Him,' won't you come?" With these words, the preacher shifts from the exhortative rhetoric of the sermon to the kinder, gentler voice of the comforter. He leaves his pulpit, steps off the platform, and puts himself in front of the Lord's Supper Table and at the level of the congregation. He extends his arms, "If you are afraid of walking that aisle, that's the way Jesus felt when he picked up the cross and started the journey to Calvary. Anything easy is not worth doing anyhow" (heard at Istrouma Baptist Church in 1985). At these words, the congregation moves from listening to singing and waits for someone among their number to leave the congregation, walk down the aisle, and into the handshake and the embrace of the preacher. There, in that personal face-to-face, private encounter, the one who seeks to know Christ as a personal savior will whisper the words of surrender to one whom the Savior has called to preach His Word.

"I am crucified," Paul said in his letter to the Galatians (chapter 2, verse 20), "I am crucified with Christ; nevertheless I live; yet not I, but Christ liveth in me."

NOTES

1. The contrast between touching and seeing the sacred versus speaking and hearing is based on observations of Catholic practices in Spanish America and of the Baptists in the American South. These observations began in 1962 and have continued to the present. As indicated in the text, some of the quoted material comes from churches in the Baton Rouge area.

A much earlier version of this paper was presented at "Ways of Speaking, Ways of Knowing," The Ethnography of Communication Conference, Portland, Oregon, April 13–15, 1992. A shortened version was part of the Key Symposium of the Southern Anthropological Society meetings, Savannah, Georgia, March 25–27, 1993. I am indebted to generous comments made at both meetings. I particularly appreciate the assistance of Jill Brody, my colleague and mentor on discourse at the Department of Geography and Anthropology, Louisiana State University, the helpful suggestions and encouragements from O. Kendall White Jr. and from Daryl White, and the patience of the Southern Baptists whenever they have heard me talk about their Christ.

2. In his fascinating discussion of orality and textuality in the composition of the Gospel of Mark, Kelber notes that the oral features present in Mark's recounting the life of Jesus diminish as Mark narrates the approaching death of Jesus. The narrative becomes more compact, obtains greater coherence, and exhibits finer temporal precision, all features of writing. Thus, writing, in its fixing of speech, appropriates death. See especially chapter 5, "Death and Life in the Word of God" (1983:184–220).

More Varieties of Religious Experience:
Time and Faith for Southern Catholics

Jon W. Anderson and Gwen Kennedy Neville

Time and constructions of time are central dimensions of religious experience and central to its variety. Conceptions of time encoded in myth and ritual project commonalities of fate and faith, and a future set apart from the diversities of present experience. Religious practices organize communities of experience with intricate and problematic associations with additional frames of time. In looking at Catholics in the contemporary South, we encountered this double complexity of temporal frames of religious experience set in institutional, personal, and intergenerational constructions and social organizations of time. From personal narratives and community gatherings, a lived logic of practice and experience—"habitus" in the term popularized by Pierre Bourdieu (1977)—emerges around temporal frames of people's lives. Here we examine experiential features of institutional, personal, and intergenerational constructions and social organizations of time that frame Catholic experience in the Bible Belt and Sunbelt Souths.[1]

Catholicism and Catholics are part of the diversity of the South, and southerners are part of the diversity of the Catholic church. Fitting the two together is frequently problematic: Catholic southerners experience being a minority both in their region and within a church denominated by other experiences. Time, how it is experienced and how one organizes it, is among the hidden dimensions of being Catholic in the South. The statements by a storekeeper in Appalachia that "knowing you're in a church that Christ founded is a great comfort" and by a Memphis businessman that "the Catholic church preserved art and culture all these centuries" both speak from a sense of institutional continuity and memory far surpassing the South's own that Catholics commonly express in this region that fetishizes its own history. At the same time, each carries more local resonances with the environment of primitive churches in Appalachia or with the bourgeois urbanity of the long-established financial and business hub of the mid-South. The regional prominence of evangelical Protestants creates contexts in which Catholic experience may be set aside from southern ones. At the same time, Catholic southerners have a second set of comparisons to their co-religionists in the urban Northeast and Midwest who set the Catholic cultural profile nationally. While Catholics in the South are immigrants like their co-religionists elsewhere in the country, the ethnic-cultural environments that sustain the "Immigrant Church" of the urban Northeast and Midwest are replaced in the South by "assimilation to the Anglo mainstream," in the words of a woman of Lebanese descent.

Similarities and differences built around liturgical and other church times and into community, family, and other secular times, we suggest, locate tensions of affirmation, identity, and recognition that compose religious experience as much as do formal beliefs and worldview. But they do so practically and through the organization of experience. Catholic churches throughout the South stand spatially and stylistically apart from mainstreet Protestant ones. Their common red-brick-and-plaster gothic style stands apart not just from the neoclassical "colonial" styles favored by Protestant churches; it stands in a period of renewed counterreformation in the nineteenth century that obliterated previous styles and was itself supplanted by more ecumenical, "modern" styles, externally indistinguishable from those of other churches and firmly anchored in the present by a modernized, less inward-turning contemporary church.

CHURCH TIMES

The salvation and redemption that set the dominant frame of time for all Christians as an irruption of the sacred into mundane time are celebrated in Catholic liturgy as a time out of time, in the mass, which reenacts the Lord's Supper and marks off participants as the original one came to be understood as superseding mortal times for immortal ones (Feeley-Harnik 1981). For Catholics, this is a moment of eternal return set apart in the flow of life that inscribes the central dialectic of World and Church that frames Catholic religiosity and experience of religion as transcendence of the mundane and the local.

In a weekly cycle punctuated by a moment of eternal time, the communicant steps apart from natural and social relations into a supernatural one. No other act of devotion or of prayer has quite this impact of separation and incorporation with the mystical body of Christ as the sacrament of communion—not stopping time such as for grace before meals nor of taking time such as for one of the Catholic church's many devotions. Space (of churches) and place (locality) are subordinated to this reenactment of the defining moment of Catholic life and experience. Protestant counterparts lack this focus of an eternal return; remembrance is their stress.

Eucharistic communion marks Catholicism as a positive act throughout the South. Church commentators note a trend toward focusing more on eucharistic communion at the expense of other devotions; but it has long been prominent in southern Catholicism. The organizational Church, with its rich repertoire of devotions and venues for expressing and focusing piety, has had a more meager and dispersed presence throughout most of the inland South by comparison to the urban Northeast and Midwest that set the norms of Catholic life in the country. Here, eucharistic communion is the core experience of Catholicism's set-apartness from the world. Its provision is tied to fierce loyalties and a history of lay-built churches, to gatherings of return and reunion that recall a past which often involved traveling long distances to attend mass.

Movement and effort are regional memories that emerge in comparisons to Catholics elsewhere—"They've had it easier, while we had to work at it," is a common sentiment—and to Protestant neighbors. They are doubly differentiating. Newcomers to the South retrace and thereby make a regional experience their own in seeking out familiar or preferred liturgical and other settings for worship, and in sometimes having to create them. Nearly all remark on having "to do more," and in so doing affirm not just a regional circumstance but a tradition of both regionalism and transcendence of regionalism in an experience that Catholics elsewhere do not share.

Attending weekend mass is a formal obligation that extends to additional Holy Days of Obligation: Christmas, Ascension, Assumption of Mary, All Saints, Immaculate Conception of Mary, Solemnity of Mary. These merge practically with a calendar of feast and celebration days on fixed and moveable dates. Holy Days, while officially continuous with the weekly obligation, are practically transitional to a second major frame of religious time, the year of the church calendar. Where the temporal frame of weekly observance inscribes the central redemptive message of Christianity in a ritual of eternal return, the complex annual frame organizes religiosity around a model of Christ's conception-birth and death-resurrection marked as sacred seasons (Advent-Christmas and Lent-Easter-Pentecost) between periods of ordinary time. By comparison with Protestant emphases on other events in the life of Christ, the repetitive emphasis of the formal church year is on the beginning and end of Christ's earthly life and the miraculous conception and assumption into heaven of Mary.

The church calendar provides a more structured and explicitly temporal frame that does not so much organize time, as weekly mass attendance does, as give a sacred, religious dimension to time. It is marked by observances with no counterparts or parallels among Catholic southerners' Protestant neighbors, such as stations of the cross in Lent, special masses on Good Friday or during Advent, midnight mass on Christmas Eve, Marian observances, and a host of others. These observances confer distinction locally and incorporation in a worldwide community of *observance* rather than Protestants' communities of association and conscience. It confers a religious meaning on the annual cycle that is additional, rather than continuous with, its meanings as a school year or fiscal year or the electoral round in the civic community.

A third frame of time is organized by the official lectionary of the Catholic church that specifies scripture readings for daily and weekly masses over a three-year period. Through this organization of passages from Old Testament, Epistles, and the Gospels for reading each day, the church as an organization reads the scriptures *for* the faithful, in the absence of a tradition of lay Bible-reading, a task that, as popularly put, is left to the clergy. Reforms associated with Vatican II have included the use of lay lectors, or readers, in the mass for the Old Testament and Epistles, but not for readings of the Gospels, which are still read with ceremony as proclamation by the priest at mass. This reform amounts to reading partly *through* rather than *to* a church reconceptualized as People of God, but it continues to affirm the organizational efficacy of offices, including those that compose the lectionary as the way to deliver scripture. Its affirmation that it takes time set apart to read the Bible has a practical impact of estranging Catholic southerners from their neighbors' Bible-reading. Set against local community is an identification with the Church Universal vested with this task. This triennial cycle is the most "churchy"—in an organizational sense—of these temporal frames. It is the most distant from ordinary lives, the most specialized, and the most distinctively Catholic.

The eternal time of eucharistic communion, the sacred times marking Christ's conception/birth and death/resurrection (and the parallel conception and assumption of Mary), and the time it takes to read the Bible inscribe three temporal frames of Catholic spirituality and identity that set them apart from their local into a translocal community that transcends mundane, passing time. "You know the same thing is happening all over the world," one put feelings of belonging to a larger civilization and setting than those of the South.

It is important that these are dimensions of *affiliation*. They do not absorb or subordinate or even mesh very well with other activities and cycles, as they might where greater density of Catholic institutions and people provide the arenas and the personnel, such as in the urban Northeast and Midwest. Instead, they confer an independent, alternative significance on time that provides points for affirmation and thus of comparison. Not everyone goes regularly to church, ponders the coming and going of Christ, and reads scripture. As ideals, someone must do them, and that is presumed to be the church, which organizes them, at least in the persons of its exemplary representatives. Archetypically, these are the clergy and members of religious orders and active lay people who are observant, "good" Catholics.

Lining up these religious frames of time retraces a practical hierarchy of Catholic affirmation from shorter temporal span or cycle to the longer. The longer the cycle, the more it is removed to the organizational Church (of clergy, religious orders and church-workers) and the less pressing it is. This precise reverse of the regional Protestant majority's hierarchy of affirmation, which proceeds from text to Christ to embodiment (as a call felt in the heart, see Harding 1987, Richardson 1990), marks Catholic priorities and gives an implicit scale of more-and-less "catholicness" against which activities, persons, and communities may be measured. The activities organized in each of these frames are universal ones, officially uninflected by local, regional, national cultural practices; as such, they form a scale of practical involvement in that world-apart and so inscribe part of the internal diversity of the Catholic world.

Obversely, the Church as an organization of clergy, officials, programs, and service institutions from missionary societies and religious orders to orphanages, hospitals, schools, and publishing houses takes care of these activities, leaving the Church Parochial to be, in local terms, more spiritual. By that is meant more focused, and more exclusively focused, on communion in perhaps the most text-minded part of the country.

INSTITUTIONAL TIME

For ordinary Catholic southerners in the interior and away from Catholic centers, this distinction can mean alienation from extended experiences of Catholicness, or bracketing what are taken to be unmarked forms as in fact regionally, institutionally, and ethnically marked forms of Catholic life. "It's not that we don't know about all that," a Catholic southerner explained about the umbra of monasteries and convents, charities and insurance societies, and the penumbra of sodalities organized by the Catholic Church; "we just never had it, or had much of it ourselves. Here, Catholics are thin on the ground. Not like the North." Statements such as this, like stories about traveling to fetch a priest or to attend a mass, surface dimensions of comparisons that respond to more practical, and less straightforwardly ideological, institutionalizations of time.

The overall comparison here is to the worlds of the Immigrant Church, to a sort of Catholic establishment with a public and cultural presence through a panoply of institutions and parallel system of activities in a successful and successfully catholicized world. In practical terms, this is largely a phenomenon of the urban Northeast and Midwest, where frames of life-time, such as for school years or stages of life, are inscribed as Catholic or in Catholic organizational terms, in an environment composed of Catholics. Catholic southerners emphasize that "faith is more a private thing here, though religion [as social identity] is sure more public." And, newcomers as well as native southerners note that "you have to work at being Catholic here, and I think that makes us appreciate it more."

The Immigrant Church is not unknown in the South. There are regional echoes and local versions of it in such places as Louisville and Mobile, and counternarratives in New Orleans and southern Louisiana. This means that older stories of being Catholic, and of Catholic success in America, are incompletely obliterated by what has become the master narrative that ties Catholic to ethnic identities. A rather different sort of experience is suggested by Margaret Mitchell, writing in the Depression-era South, making her iconic southern heroine of *Gone with the Wind* an Irish Catholic in Atlanta. Ethnicity, but not immigrant past, is obliterated under the twin pressures of overriding racial classification and by "assimilation to the Anglo mainstream," as a woman of Lebanese descent put it, that restrict the possibilities of alternative communities. Catholic identity is assimilated instead to the regional trophology of family, pioneering, and individual journeys. "I'm a mongrel dog," a Tennessee executive and former state legislator put it in a practiced story of wandering ancestors making fresh starts in each generation.

The Immigrant Church, which became a master narrative of Catholic America, fits awkwardly the experiences and memory of Catholic southerners. This model for relating to a larger whole supplanted previous models from the early days of the republic, colonial Maryland or, more problematically, those of French Louisiana or the Spanish mission West. As the dominant frame of modern American-Catholic historiography apart from institutional church history, its themes of struggle and success tend to stall on struggle when applied to the South (e.g., Nolan 1987). In place of success followed by assimilation, a trophology of suffering and isolation historically became badges of Catholicism in the South. Southerners, Flannery O'Connor (1969) reminds us, are no strangers to suffering and defeat; Catholicism's rich theology of suffering may resonate with the South's own overwrought senses of defeat and subjugation and has for curmudgeonly intellectuals such as Walker Percy and Alan Tate. But where Tate and Percy were moved by anachronism, contemporary Catholic southerners move to synchronize recent modernization of church (with Vatican II) and region (with civil rights). McDonogh (1993) has drawn out the image of pictures of John F. Kennedy alongside those of Pope John XXIII in black Catholic households in Savannah. A similar sentiment was put, in Appalachia, as "mainstreaming" as both Catholics and southerners within America.

The history of church and region intersect in narratives that, by comparison, balance their traditions awkwardly. Catholics appear as missionaries, pioneers, and builders in church-written history. Throughout such histories (e.g., McNally 1987), senses of newness give way to sojourn in a body of literature written about rather than by Catholic south-

erners. Alternative histories are inscribed—often literally—in buildings, from the comparatively modest cathedrals of southern dioceses
that are repositories for the life of a Catholic community, to the red-brick
gothic and baroque churches of southern river towns that memorialize
Catholic social arrival and obliterate simpler chapels, often lay-built,
of the pioneer period. Southern parishes register histories of rebuilding and relocation as successions of often-simple pioneer beginnings by
later institutional arrival, and success as transition from lay to clerical
foundation and denomination of religious life.

The pull and tug of religion with the world, which all religions would
reform to some degree and Christian ones would ultimately transcend,
is acted out in Catholic terms as a long-running drama that affirms a
sense of spirituality marked by patience. "That's just the way he is," remarked a woman about her bishop's abrupt departure from a celebration
following the consecration of their new chapel: "He's a busy man, but
we'll get him trained." By comparison, Protestant anxieties (in sensi-
bilities anticipating apocalypse at any time) are bridged not by patience
but, for denominations originating in dissent, by tolerance. The difference is relative, but important: tolerance or freedom of conscience
in more explicitly theological terms implies a different spirituality than
patience. Carol Greenhouse (1986:45) recounts the testimony of a born-
again Baptist in Georgia who found Jesus at the moment of determining
to divorce her ne'er-do-well husband and decided to stay with her marriage. In her testimony, Jesus helped her to see and accept differences
with her husband, to have, as Greenhouse puts it, both her marriage and
her divorce because "[he] is not saved, and I am. I'm going to heaven
and he's going to hell."

The first woman's comment on her bishop, like the history of rebuilding and relocating churches, marks the intersection of different
rhythms of local community with bureaucratic times of the organizational church. These dimensions take on meanings and functions that
have more to do with institutional affirmation that are complemented,
extended, and variously overlapping with others. As alternatives, they
are glossed in an American idiom of choice as well as in Catholic idioms
of tensions between a World of the Church and Church in the World.
Traveling distance is spending time just to get to church and part of
the experience, as is waiting for priests who rotate among dispersed
parishes. So is money and effort invested in building and rebuilding

churches, and a tradition-minded disinclination to Bible study in the one region of America where the Bible is the most studied and quoted of texts. These underlay ways they read and read into experiences that are not themselves religious in a formal sense.

COMMUNITY AND FAMILY TIME

Community time for southern Catholics is more than the history of the parish. Religious community intersects with and is integral to family time in the South for Catholic and Protestant alike. Neville (1987) earlier identified a complex of family reunions, church homecomings and anniversaries, cemetery association days, and denominational summer communities in which Protestant southerners constructed a meaning system merging family with religion. It is a complex in which extended families descended of honored ancestors often overlap with founders of local church congregations, which are ritually joined in kin-religious gatherings. Their high ceremonial time is summer, when these gatherings are held, with vast numbers of people assembling from scattered residences to sites that enfold family and church in a community of faith organized by a community of kin.

Catholic gatherings in the South also mobilize a pattern of family and community time that includes reunions, church anniversaries, and other gatherings based on kinship, to enclose Catholic religious imperatives within the rhythms of community and lifecycle. Family times are, as for Protestants, summer times; in the Catholic church calendar, this is Ordinary Time, not keyed to liturgical holy seasons. In practice, this time is semisacralized throughout the South by family-focused activities (reunions, vacations, attendance at religious conference centers). Family- and parish-historical (e.g., anniversary) events fall into this season partly because of their absence of formal church liturgical significance. In a kind of inversion of the sacred, family time, which is subordinated in the formal calendar to church time, rises and enfolds church through the work of symbolic and ritual vocabularies of family time.

Catholic family and community time, then, play in a double set of tensions with community time of the surrounding society and with church times. The two cross and absorb each other. Baptisms, confirmations, weddings, anniversaries of marriages, and funerals punctuate the formal liturgical year that absorbs them into church time. But in summertime gatherings for reunions, parish picnics, and fall fairs, church assimilated to family (in its sacred time) as one of its activities. In a parish gathering held on its particular namesake saint's day, a mass is the religious focal point, symbolically placing the company within Catholicism's most embracive time, and the one they share with each other. But the relationship is inverted in subsequent festivity that celebrates community and kinship through dinner provided by parishioners and by singing, dancing, games, and enjoyment in the company of assembled family and friends, for which women are the liturgical specialists. Often, such events are fundraisers, further incorporating church into family, or reversing the patronage, protection, and sponsorship. It is a mark of pride that such events attract non-Catholic neighbors, who thereby turn it into a community affair and acknowledge their neighbors' church as part of the community.

When asked what was happening in parishes in the summer, the answer was often "nothing." "Nothing" in this context refers to church-based activities and to parish as church but not as a community. This is a time when family and community "take over" symbolically and practically what is given over to church at other times.

Catholic experience in the South includes experience of different rhythms and meanings of time, some of which unite them with other Catholics, some with both broader history, and some with more local southern experiences. These frames include liturgical times that unite virtual communities of faith and belief, and their variable institutionalization as a dimension of differentiation from the world and within a world imagined by the Church. Liturgical times extend into institutional times with additional practical dimensions comparing regions and kinds of community. Other frames include personal and group experiences in more local, less transient (and transcendent) communities of shared memory and experience. In the South, these tend to be family frames instead of those of ethnic communities that elsewhere are fused with Catholic stories. Tensions between and within these frames become variable dimensions of religious experience.

We see in the play of these frames multiple conceptions and experiences that play against each other and inscribe a double complexity of being Catholic and southern. Time is socially organized, but also experienced through practices that Pierre Bourdieu (1977), following Mauss (1950), called "habitus." This concept shifts analytical focus from replication and complementation of forms to wider, often vaguer but more immediate—in this case temporal—frames of experience. Temporal frames that belong to liturgical time and those that belong to personal and community times articulate differentiations, whose phases or phrases variably intersect others to compose historical parts of the experience of Catholic southerners. These intersections inscribe tensions locally between natural communities and virtual communities, which are translocal in time as well as in space. It is in institutional strains toward virtual community and the activation of natural communities that Catholic southerners are differentiated from and united with other Catholics and other southerners at the level not just of religious identity or expression but also of religious experience. Focusing on temporal frames permits us to see this double complexity in the tensions within and between activities, and extends the move from the social settings of religious identity (e.g., Tyson, Peacock, and Patterson 1988) to those of religious expression a further step to the social dimensions of religious experience.

NOTE

1. This paper is based on a research project, "Cultural Differences of Bible Belt Catholics," supported by a grant from the Catholic Church Extension Society to the Catholic University of America. Jon Anderson, Gwen Kennedy Neville, and Gary McDonogh collaborated in a comparative ethnographic study of contemporary Catholic communities in Appalachia and the Mississippi Delta, Georgia and Florida, and northern Louisiana and central Texas; Daniel Ruff undertook a comparative study of Catholic and Protestant preaching in North Carolina; and Paul Murray conducted an analysis of Catholic writing about the church in the South. We have all benefited from advice and comments on the progress of the project from Sam Hill, Miles Richardson, James Peacock, and others, most especially our hosts who shared with us their experiences, views, and events.

"Give Me That Old-Time Religion": The Genealogy and Cultural Politics of an Afro-Christian Celebration in Halifax County, North Carolina

Faye V. Harrison

During Labor Day weekend (September 5–6) in 1992, more than two hundred descendants of Susan Brown, and especially of her eldest son, the Reverend Burgess Harper, and his wife, Tempie Blount Harper, gathered for a family reunion in Halifax County, North Carolina. This rural county was the place where, in the aftermath of slavery and the Civil War, the founders of the postbellum Harper family and their extended kindred joined forces with their neighbors to build and, in the hostile post-Reconstruction climate, defend a community of African American freedpeople. The reunion pilgrimage brought kinspeople living all over the United States back to their foreparents' North Carolinian home to celebrate their ancestors' struggles, sacrifices, and accomplishments and to recall and highlight the religiously informed cultural and sociopolitical values and practices that marked the lifeways of the "old-time folk" who came up from the darkness of slavery toward the light of freedom.

Among other things, this North Carolina reunion reassessed and renegotiated the meaning of "family" and "kinship" for dispersed folk who, for the most part, go about their everyday lives in postindustrial America in the context of one or, at most, two concentric inner circles of family, that is, the immediate nuclear family plus grandparents, parents' siblings, and first cousins. The return "home" to Halifax provided a symbolically charged cultural context for the articulation and regeneration of a "sentiment of corporateness" connecting both close and distant relatives who share a common sense of origin and a common "sense of place" (Wiggins 1987:79), linking them to the original home-site (the 125-acre Harper farm) and to Pleasant Grove Baptist Church, one of the country churches Rev. Harper founded across a four-county radius in Halifax, Warren, Nash, and Franklin counties.

The corporateness that is revitalized through ritually significant down-home family reunions provides an important source of grounding for the sense of cultural tradition that is an integral feature of the life of rural North Carolina migrants and their urban offspring in cities across the country. In the inner-city Washington, D.C., neighborhood of Elm Valley, Brett Williams (1988) observed that Carolina traditions of gardening, reciprocal exchange of medicines and foodstuffs, fishing, and feasting were refashioned and reinvented. She argues that "Carolina culture helps black residents . . . construct alternative identities and relationships based on ties of friendship and family, history and place. This symbolic anchor is not without contradictions, given the true grimness of some of the areas former Carolinians have left behind. Nonetheless, in many ways it is a powerfully negotiated oppositional identity, which knits together neighbors and draws families together across the city" (3).

Williams claims that the social identity anchored in this shared sense of cultural traditions facilitates resistance to mass-mediated messages about the commodification of contemporary American life and the place of racially subordinated blacks in the life of the nation. This identity embedded in cultural resistance informs how Carolina kin in the various urban settings in which they live reinvent community and invest meaning in both private and public life.

The Harper family reunion was more than just an expression of family values and solidarity. Grafted onto the Labor Day national holiday, with its characteristic focus on the rights and accomplishments of labor in American society, were both an ancestor-focused pilgrimage and an emancipation celebration of the legally sanctioned freedom of all blacks as "fictive kin" (Fordham 1988). The labor being ritually recognized that long holiday weekend was that of freed and free black labor, that of the African American labor force that knows at least through the transgenerational memory embedded in family traditions the brutality and dehumanization of slavery. As a set of Labor Day weekend kinship ritual events, the Harper family reunion synthesized elements of the traditional mid-to-late-summer emancipation celebrations that have become a salient feature of African American culture across the United States (Wiggins 1987).

This essay examines the Harper family reunion as an emancipation celebration combining sacred and secular rituals at three historically and symbolically salient local sites: Pleasant Grove Baptist Church (founded by Burgess Harper and a symbol of his role as a "divine" and civic leader), Master's Economy Inn (a white-owned and managed hotel, a symbol of the "master's big house"), and the grounds of the original homestead—the family land that is the spiritual home for the living and dead Harper kin (Carnegie 1987). According to the ensuing analysis, the Labor Day weekend celebration dramatized the continuing significance of all of the phases of the historic African American saga—the African past, slavery, emancipation, and the ongoing struggle for social equality and freedom since formal emancipation (Wiggins 1987:49).

CELEBRATING THROUGH WORSHIP,
FELLOWSHIP, ENTERTAINMENT, AND PLAY

Generally, emancipation celebrations fall into three basic categories: (1) those emphasizing religious thanksgiving with praying, singing, and preaching; (2) those devoted to the "carnal good times" with their "culinary rituals of eating barbecue and drinking whiskey to excess as well as . . . singing, dancing, and playing games"; and (3) those that combine these two traditions, accommodating a wide cross-section of the "lost and saved" (Wiggins 1987:34, 35, 36). The Harper family reunion represents an emancipation celebration of the third category, one that synthesizes sacred and secular dimensions and embodies Afro-Christian religious sentiments, political interests and concerns, expressions of civic responsibility, and a penchant for playful fun.

The Memorial Service in the Sacred Space of
Pleasant Grove Baptist Church: Church History

Pleasant Grove Baptist Church was founded in 1882 during a period of intense and violently racist white backlash against the Reconstruction policies that "[attempted] to create, for the first time in our history, an interracial democracy" (Foner 1993:118). According to the church's 104th anniversary album, Burgess Harper "started [the church] under a bush arbor" in response to a calling from God. "With bushes, limbs, and tree branches for the church's ceiling, rocks for the church's pews, and the bare ground for the church's floor, Rev. Harper with his band of followers had their first service in their new church." By 1905 a building had been erected "where the members could worship and not be hindered because of rain, storms, snow, or the bitter cold as was the case in trying to worship under the bush arbor" (Pleasant Grove Baptist Church 1986:11).

The narrative on the church history begins with Burgess Harper's birth in 1850. This means that the church traces its religious and cultural genealogy to the days of slavery, when, as the church historian stated: "Burgess Harper . . . witnessed daily the cruel and inhumane treatment . . . the slaves had to endure. Prayers were offered daily by the slaves that the Lord, their God, would send a proclamation to them as He had to Moses thousands of years before when he commanded . . . Moses to go down to Egypt and set His people free. Black slaves around Essex, Hollister and Halifax were praying that God would once again make a proclamation that His people would be set free" (Pleasant Grove Baptist Church 1986:11).

The narrative goes on to recount that on 1 January 1863 Abraham Lincoln issued the Emancipation Proclamation. This momentous event was construed to be an answer to the slaves' prayers for freedom. While Lincoln is depicted as God's medium, a symbolic Moses, in Pleasant Grove's narrative of origin (as well as that of another church), Burgess Harper is cast as the more immediate, local prophet and "divine leader" (Odell Baptist Church 1978) who established not only a church (or churches) but the central, multifunctional institutional nexus of a wider community within which African American freedpeople struggled against great odds to make their lives as emergent citizens meaningful. The sociocultural forces shaping the formation of social identity, the regulation of family life, economic cooperation and mutual aid, sociopolitical action, and healing and the maintenance of health were harnessed within the institutional context of the church.

Pleasant Grove was only one of several churches for which Rev. Harper was responsible over the course of his more than fifty-year ministry. Although he preached at St. John, Social Union, and Union Hill in

Nash County; at Guilfield Baptist in Franklin County; at Odell in eastern Warren County; and at Bear Swamp and Pine Chapel in Halifax, Pleasant Grove was the Harper family's home church, located within easy traveling distance from the homestead where Burgess and his helpmate, Tempie Blount Harper, farmed and raised seven sons and two daughters (Harper 1931).

Emancipation Ritual of Thanksgiving: Fellowship/Hospitality Hour
(Saturday 11:00 A.M.–12:30 P.M.)

The worship service on Saturday, 5 September was preceded by an informal period of hospitality and fellowship in the multipurpose room behind the altar and sanctuary. These interactions and communications were casual and spontaneous, allowing relatives who grew up together to reacquaint themselves and those who were strangers to be introduced and become more familiar. This prelude to the memorial service extended the boundaries of kinship to encompass more distant and unfamiliar kin who share Rev. Burgess Harper and/or his mother Susan Brown as common ancestors.

While the overwhelming majority of the celebrants were Burgess Harper's descendants, three of the celebrants were descendants of Susan Brown's other offspring. The fact that only three or so persons representing the Brown branch of the extended family were present is perhaps a reflection of the extent to which familial segmentation (Jones 1980) had separated or distanced the two divergent lines of descent. Interestingly, this segmentation is symbolically represented by the distinctions made by a ninety-one-year-old granddaughter of Burgess and Tempie, Florence Harper Boney, when she viewed a 1930s family photograph of Susan, five of her offspring, three of her grandchildren, and one great-grandchild. The elderly woman voluntarily designated Burgess Harper and "Aunt Lucy"—a woman whom none of the others present could identify—as Susan Brown's "slave-born" son and daughter, and John, Alex, and Eliza Brown as her "free-born" offspring. Assuming that her mode of expression was more than idiosyncratic, it appears that these categories were significant ones for characterizing members of the transitional generation bordering slavery and freedom. The slave-free distinction between the two sets of offspring is also reinforced by the fact that the Harpers and Browns were half-siblings. Moreover, the former slaves, Lucy and Burgess Harper, were born out of wedlock as the progeny of a slave master who exercised his masculinist power over his female property. Susan's extreme vulnerability as an enslaved woman is reflected in the sexual exploitation and violation that resulted in Burgess's and Lucy's births. Although clearly respected and admired for her fortitude and longevity (having lived for about 113 years), "Grandma Susan's" experience as a victim of slavery's carnal violence may have precluded her from becoming the focal ancestor, genealogical apex, and cultural heroine around which the descent group was organized. In other words, Burgess Harper may have been a more fitting symbol of postslavery and postemancipation hopes and dreams because of his unblemished role-model status as an esteemed religious figure, who came of age as a freed man and developed into a proactive subject and historical agent, and who begot all of his children with the blessings of holy Christian matrimony. In more concrete, practical terms, the segmentation between the Harper and Brown branches may also have been the outcome of divergent out-migration patterns. While the bulk of the Browns migrated to Georgia and Virginia, a larger critical mass of the Harper descendants remained in North Carolina to carry on the family traditions and to reinforce their concrete and symbolic connections with the family home, church, and community.

Inspirational Memorial Worship Service (Saturday, 12:30 P.M.–1:30 P.M.)

With instrumental and vocal musical performances, prayers, the lighting of ancestral candles, presentations about the various branches of the extended family, a sermon by a contemporary Reverend Harper (one of the original Reverend Harper's grandsons), and a benediction by the current pastor of the church, the kindred gave thanks for the blessings and gifts bestowed on the ancestors as well as the generations of descendants. The short speeches that the organizers of the event and six representatives of family branches delivered highlighted the progress and successes of the black American dream. In the context of this dream, as articulated best by Martin Luther King Jr., individual achievements—accomplished despite the obstacles racism imposes— were presented as the fulfillment of familywide goals. Special emphasis was placed on educational attainment (winning scholarships, graduating from college), occupational mobility (acquiring good jobs), and political involvement (voting, being active Democratic party supporters, and belonging to the NAACP). The arduous climb from the indignities of slavery to the achievements of late twentieth-century life was dramatically recounted through direct statements in speeches as well as through indirect references in song lyrics and in the binary opposition implicit in the success and thanksgiving narratives of the various family branches.

According to the memorial service oratory, through faith in God, hard work, and commitment to family, Burgess and Tempie Harper became self-taught, respectable citizens who set a profound example for the generations that followed them. Due to the piety that Burgess and Tempie Harper taught through their words and deeds, descendants who remained in Halifax County are represented among the successful farmers and small business proprietors, in the public school system as both teachers and support staff, and in the leadership of the Halifax County Democratic Party. And descendants residing elsewhere are represented across an even wider cross-section of occupations and social roles. The importance assigned to political participation was emphasized by directing special attention to a relative in Philadelphia who serves as a "legislative/regulatory affairs monitor" with Philadelphia's Minority Business Enterprise Council. This man's profile was further delineated in the Harper Family Newsletter (1992), which pinpointed that he "meets regularly with members of the small business committee on Capitol Hill." Without explicitly campaigning for the Democratic party, the ceremony pointed to the importance of the then-upcoming 1992 national election as a means of bringing the conservative sociopolitical climate of the Reagan and Bush administrations to a close. In keeping with longstanding tradition, the memorial service, like emancipation celebrations generally, provided a forum for protest and other kinds of political statements (Wiggins 1987:109). Good citizenship, projected as a family virtue, was also exhibited within the family before the civil rights and post–civil rights eras. In view of the centrality of the church in black community life, Burgess Harper served as a leader in both sacred and secular realms. Celebrants were reminded of the example set by Robert Henry Harper, the son whose descendants continue to live at the homeplace and whose offspring have accepted the responsibility for coordinating the reunions. Henry "kept up with political happenings and encouraged his friends to register, vote, and keep aware of racial and political fairness. In 1950 he became a charter member of the Wayman-Enfield branch of the NAACP" (Harper Family 1989:10). Henry, Burgess and Tempie's eighth child, was also a model parent who combined farming with teaching school and encouraged his children to attain as much education as possible. Possibly in his memory as much as in that of his father, who founded the first school for black children in the Essex-Hollister area, a scholarship fund committee was established to mark the 1992 reunion and the values/goals it represented.

The memorial service was a ritual of thanksgiving that focused celebrants' attention on both the struggles of the ancestral past and the achievements and ongoing goals of the present. Faith in God, educational attainment, and political participation were highlighted as vehicles for family stability, social mobility, economic security, and racial equality.

The Banquet at Master's Economy Inn: Appropriating the
"Master's Big House" (Saturday, 2:30 P.M.)

After the sacred memorial service, the celebrants traveled to the secular banquet site, Master's Economy Inn. There the communicants of the secular communion ate a varied selection of professionally prepared foods while seated at white cloth-covered tables. While eating, the celebrants listened to more speeches, witnessed an African dance, and played games of family-focused trivial pursuit. Although a secular rite of commensality, the banquet integrated praying for blessings and a tribal dance that in its original indigenous context probably represented an animist religious rite. The performance of a pagan or heathen dance took place in this secularized setting as entertainment for a devout Christian audience. Interestingly, the earthy, sensual African dance was performed inside a white-controlled, contractual setting rather than outside in a space designated as black-centered and communal, such as the homeplace outside of Essex. According to the views of some of the celebrants, such a dance rite probably made the masters of the antebellum past as well as those who internalized their values "roll over in their graves." And this may very well have been the intention at this black ancestor–focused celebration of kinship. African blackness, once ideologically constructed as the antithesis to genteel, civilized, and free whiteness, was brought straight into the "master's" dining room where black presence was historically expected to be reserved, servile, "seen and not heard," and probably barely seen at all. In other words, in the white master's house the black slave was supposed to be an object rather than a subject.

The adolescent girls dancing to the traditional African polyrhythmic beat of tape-recorded drumming were highly visible, expressive, and demonstrative as African American *subjects* revitalized by the retrieval and reinvention of their distinctively African cultural heritage. They seemed to express the idea that the Harper descendants should claim their identity as *African* Americans, not Negroes, not even blacks, and certainly not the "neither Black nor White" social dilemma experienced by Alex Haley's grandmother Queen (Haley and Stevens 1993) and probably by Burgess Harper, who, although clearly committed to the Negro, Black, Afro-American, and/or African American community, was indeed socially constructed as a biracial being who could never forget the pain of having been begotten in part by a biological genitor but not by an authentic sociocultural father. In the historical context of his life, a peculiar fatherless-son dilemma informed his and many other mulattoes' negotiation of racial selfhood.

That process of identity formation occurred in the circumstances of post-Reconstruction Halifax County. That particular context was complicated by the existence of not only black and white communities, but of intermediate categories such as "issues" (called "Ishies" in the vernacular) or those descended from "free issues" rather than slaves, and Indians (Haliwa-Saponi) who are reputed to have triracial origins and kinship connections with issue, black, and white communities. And as already implied, within the black community there was a substantial proportion of mixed bloods of both biracial and triracial origins. Racial identities were negotiated in this complex context. The mulatto identity of many turn-of-the-century African Americans eventually withered away into a generalized, inclusive blackness shared by the majority of those who trace their freedom to the emancipation of the mid-1860s.

The African dance was a marker of an unambiguously African American social identity and status, differentiating the extended Harper family from those within Halifax—and perhaps within the kindred as well —who would claim Indianness or near-whiteness. At any family reunion before the Second Reconstruction (Marable 1984) of the post–World War II and civil rights era, African dancing or any expression of Africanness would probably have been inconceivable and objectionable in a climate where color consciousness and claims of biracial origins were more commonplace. But in 1992 inside the banquet hall of Master's Economy Inn, the subversive assertion of an African past and a neo-African present was a well-received youthful performance that symbolically appropriated what in the past had been claimed as the master's property, namely the bodies and souls of black folk as well as the interior space of the master's big house. Through the drama of dance, the contents and contours of Harper family racial identity were reshaped in the vision of the younger generation.

The Pig Pickin' at the Old Homeplace (Sunday Afternoon Long)

The formality of the banquet in the enclosure of Master's Economy Inn can be sharply contrasted with the casual outdoor setting of the Sunday afternoon pig pickin' or barbecue, where games and play defined the style and tone of interaction and communication on the communal grounds of the historic homeplace. The smells, sights, and tastes of barbecue—mostly pork but some chicken—defined this occasion as one in which celebrants could eat "high on the hog" and reenact their foreparents' or their own pastoral childhood (Wiggins 1987:79–83). The playful outdoor frolicking of the pig pickin' recreated the symbolic conditions of childhood and of down-home for celebrants of all ages, most of whom were encouraged to "make pigs of themselves" and participate in the family olympic games. Through participating in the walking relay, potato race, three-legged race, basketball shoot, and horseshoes, celebrants competed both individually and in teams for athletic distinction and/or for recognition as comic relief. The sight of older relatives racing alongside more agile and coordinated youngsters in potato sacks signaled a form of social leveling, relegating adults to honorary "kids for a day" status. Leveling and the solidarity that can be associated with equality were also manifest in the distribution and wearing of family reunion T-shirts, which served as a uniform of unification.

Besides reconstructing the boundaries of the communal body of kin through the secular rites of eating good food and playing games, celebrants also took advantage of the afternoon gathering to begin plans for future extended family activities, such as the scholarship fund for deserving and needy college-bound students within the family, the establishment of a more regular newsletter, and plans for conscripting

someone to write the family history. The socializing at the pig pickin'
provided an occasion for recruiting new organizers to collaborate with
and eventually replace those, mostly women, who had assumed the
responsibility for maintaining the family reunion tradition and the sense
of extended kinship with which it is associated.

Although the locus of a secular event, the homeplace is also of special spiritual significance. It represents the site where the present meets
the past, where the cultivators sowed and reaped the fruits of their
free labor, and where Burgess Harper sang farewell songs of religious
and social commentary with his sons to mark their migration to New
York State, Baltimore, and Norfolk. The homeland symbolizes freedom, family, and the fulfillment of God's promise to Burgess when he
followed the calling he received to preach His Word. The fruits of spiritual and practical labor are, therefore, embodied in the Harper family
land. Consequently, the pig pickin' was grounded in the intersection or
conjuncture of secular and sacred fields of meaning and practice.

THE CULTURAL POLITICS OF AFRO-CHRISTIAN CELEBRATION

Family reunion, church homecoming, and emancipation celebrations
ritualistically define a shared sense of origin, place, and corporateness within extended kindreds and often wider communities. The social
identity anchored in the normative principles of corporate kinship—
in both consanguineal and fictive senses of the concept—informs the
meanings and practices of everyday life for kinfolk in Carolina and
everywhere they are dispersed.

The saga of the Harper family that is ritually reenacted at periodic
family reunions symbolizes the general historical experience of African Americans as an oppressed people, from their origins in Africa,
through the transatlantic middle passage to southern U.S. plantation
slavery, through emancipation and the volatile racist backlash against
it, through the post–World War II struggles that gave rise to the Second Reconstruction period, and to the aftermath of that Second Reconstruction as experienced in 1992 and today. The Harper family reunion
was organized to provide inspiration and refocused vision for mus-
tering the cultural resilience and creativity necessary for renegotiating
the parameters of freedom and citizenship at this challenging historical juncture—which is for many African Americans (whether farmers,

workers, members of the middle class, or the chronically unemployed) a period of intense social and economic crisis. The family reunion represented a medium for recalling members of the kindred to reproduce in their lives and experiences the religiously informed social and political struggles for full humanity and social equality in which Burgess and Tempie Harper engaged throughout their exemplary lives. The reunion dramatized the continuing relevance of the biblically informed exodus of African Americans from bondage to legal emancipation and beyond. The family reunion and emancipation celebration provide a window through which to observe how the spiritual and sociopolitical meanings of freedom, racial and ethnic identity, and American citizenship have been and are continually being contested, renegotiated, and redefined.

NOTE

I would not have been able to write this essay without the inspiration, assistance, and support I received from Odelia Harper Harrison, Pearl Hamilton Harper, Claudia Harper Brinkley, and William Conwill. I also thank my colleagues Yvonne Jones and Benita Howell for their helpful suggestions and encouragement. I dedicate this essay to the memory of my grandparents, Arthur and Tola Harper, who left Halifax County, North Carolina, in the mid-1920s for Norfolk, Virginia, and brought with them an undying sense of origin and corporate kinship. That kinship-mediated ethos helped shape the identity of their grandchildren, some of whom have become family reunion celebrants and pilgrims.

In addition to the printed documents identified in the references, this research is based on telephone conversations and correspondence with Pearl Harper and Claudia Harper Brinkley, a taped interview with the late Arthur Harper Sr., and participant observation.

The Role of Christianity in the Snowbird Cherokee Community

Sharlotte Neely

I suppose the first time I met Billy Fourkiller from Oklahoma must have been in 1973, because at the Trail of Tears Singing in 1974 I knew enough to snap a slide of him and ask him some questions. By 1978 he was dead. And in the summer of 1990 my family and I attended the Billy Fourkiller Singing, tucked away down a dirt road on a grassy hillside in the twilight of the Snowbird Mountains of North Carolina.

Cherokee Edna Chickalillie hosted the event that had attracted more than a hundred spectators. Not as large a crowd, I thought, as those at the older Trail of Tears Singings, and not as many Oklahoma Cherokees. But I did see many old friends from Snowbird, such as the Longs and Jacksons, and there were the usual visitors from the main reservation fifty miles away and from the surrounding white communities. We bought some hot dogs and cokes from the concession stand and settled down to enjoy the parade of gospel singers who performed atop the makeshift, wooden stage.

Amid the joyous music of Christianity I heard only one negative comment from anyone. When a white Georgia woman took the stage to sing and identified herself to the audience as Cherokee, a young Snowbird Cherokee woman turned to me and whispered scornfully, "Now that's a 'wannabee.'"

"Wannabees" and "white Indians" do not typically receive much respect from the traditionalist Cherokees of Graham County's Snowbird community. Snowbird Cherokees would rather interact with other "real Indians" from Oklahoma, or even with whites for that matter. For the largely fullblood, Cherokee language–speaking traditionalists of communities such as Snowbird, or even Big Cove on the main reservation, wannabees and white Indians represent a threat to Cherokee identity, Cherokee culture, the Cherokee land base, and the Cherokee economy. The only difference between wannabees and white Indians in the minds of traditionalists is that white Indians are already legally enrolled as North Carolina Cherokees and wannabees would like to be enrolled. Recently the state of Georgia has even given state recognition to groups that many North Carolina Cherokees claim are not real Indians.

Since the removal of 1838, Christian churches have served as the major institutions preserving Cherokee traditionalism in North Carolina. It is not a little ironic that the churches, introduced by missionaries aiming to change Cherokee culture, have functioned as much as agents of cultural persistence as acculturation.

In 1848 traveler Charles Lanman noted that the North Carolina Cherokees were mostly Baptists and Methodists. At the church service he attended, the sermon and the singing were both in the Cherokee language (Lanman 1849:95). Ultimately, Southern Baptist became the major religion among Cherokees, probably for at least two reasons. Baptists practiced total immersion baptisms, which reminded early converts of similar water purification rites in their native religion. Also, Baptist churches were not so hierarchical as to demand outside white ministers. The Cherokees liked having Cherokee preachers and running their own churches.

Today Snowbird is the most traditional of the Cherokee communities. Snowbird still has a higher percentage of fullbloods and Cherokee language speakers than any other North Carolina Cherokee community, although in the last twenty years, as I have observed the community, both blood degree and Cherokee speakers have declined. There are also still traditional crafts, practitioners of native medicine, and a value system based on harmony.

Aiding efforts to preserve Indian identity, the language, and the value system are the Snowbird churches. Three of the four churches in the community of nearly four hundred people are Baptist and have functioned in Cherokee control for decades. Buffalo Baptist mostly uses English in its services. Many of the first whites to intermarry into the Snowbird community attend Buffalo Baptist with their families. Zion Hill Baptist uses both English and Cherokee. The Trail of Tears Gospel Singing is organized each summer by the members of Zion Hill. Little

Snowbird Baptist attempts to use the Cherokee language exclusively. That church recently erected a large cross bearing the first line of the Twenty-third Psalm written in both English and Cherokee.

The fourth church, the interdenominational Church of the Lamb, was founded in the late 1980s by a white missionary. That church elicits ambivalent feelings from Snowbird's residents. As good Christians, Snowbird Cherokees from all three Baptist churches volunteered time toward the actual construction of the Church of the Lamb. Some residents privately expressed resentment, however, that their community would be targeted as in need of Christian missionaries to preach to them. Outside whites are not resented in helping roles. In fact, while at the Billy Fourkiller Singing, I met a white woman from Atlanta whose church has given financial aid to Little Snowbird Baptist and to a Snowbird college scholarship fund. The problem seems to focus on who is to be in control. For more than a century, Snowbird churches have had Indian preachers and used the Cherokee language. Whites have always been welcome to attend, but not to control, these Indian churches.

Long before local schools were integrated in the 1950s and 1960s and long before Indians could hold jobs alongside whites, Snowbird's Indian churches functioned in the dual role of bringing whites and Indians together and as institutions exclusively in Indian control. The churches were built, run, and financed by their Indian members; their ministers were Indians who preached in the Cherokee language; their choirs and congregations sang in Cherokee; their services included pre-Christian Cherokee myths reinterpreted as parables of Jesus; and the style of their church services conformed to a Cherokee value system in which talk of harmony and generosity were more important than accusations of sin.

Yet whites were always welcome to attend, and these Indian churches organized Sunday afternoon gospel singings that attracted many white visitors. In fact, the first white-Indian intermarriage in Snowbird, in the early 1960s, between Ned and Shirley Long, happened because the couple met at such a church singing.

In 1968 the first three-day, outdoor gospel event, the Trail of Tears Singing, was held along the banks of Snowbird Creek near Zion Hill Baptist Church. A Snowbird minister, the Reverend Ikey Jackson, had chanced to attend a large Trail of Tears Singing in Oklahoma and was so inspired that he resolved to begin a similar ceremony in North Carolina, a goal he accomplished before his untimely death in 1972. The Trail of Tears Singing in the Snowbird community has been so successful in attendance and financially that by the summer of 1990, in addition to the Trail of Tears Singing, three more multiday, outdoor singings were held, including the Billy Fourkiller Singing, named for the late Oklahoma Cherokee singer who performed at all the early Trail of Tears Singings. Oklahoma Cherokees attended all four singings in 1990.

Two characteristics are most notable about Cherokee participants at a religious event such as the Trail of Tears Singing: for the most part, the participants are fundamentalist Christians, and they are also fluent Cherokee-language speakers. The first of these characteristics is indicative of their degree of acculturation and their identity with many Americans and especially with their white Appalachian neighbors in the South. Because of this acculturation, the Trail of Tears Singing is a good example of interethnic relations. The second characteristic symbolizes the degree to which North Carolina's Eastern Cherokees have retained crucial Cherokee traits and identity as a Native American ethnic group and with Oklahoma's Western Cherokees. Because of this, the singing is a good example of intertribal relations. At the Trail of Tears Singing, it is possible to observe Snowbird Cherokees interacting with people from other Eastern Cherokee communities, Eastern Cherokees in general interacting with Western Cherokees, and Indians interacting with whites.

The Trail of Tears Singing, which Zion Hill Baptist Church organizes every summer, is a direct result and one of the better examples of continued contact between North Carolina and Oklahoma Cherokees. The ceremony is named for the route, the Trail of Tears, over which approximately sixteen thousand Cherokee Indians were forcibly marched to Indian Territory (now Oklahoma) in the winter of 1838 and 1839. Removed from their homes at gunpoint by southern militiamen and the U.S. Army and held in stockades for weeks or months, at least four thousand Cherokees died of disease, exposure, malnutrition, starvation, and murder during or immediately before the removal march. The death rate was particularly high among the children, and numerous deaths must have occurred every day of the march. The continual mourning christened the route the "Trail of Tears," a route lined with thousands of unmarked graves. The Trail of Tears is a real and a symbolic link between the two major populations of Cherokee Indians, those in North Carolina and those in Oklahoma. It is thus appropriate that two religious ceremonies that annually reunite the Cherokees should be named after the Trail of Tears. It is, after all, necessary for each group to retrace the trail in order to join the other body of people, and for the Cherokees in Oklahoma, it is the path back to their ancestral homeland. The Trail of Tears serves as a reminder that the Cherokees, although in 1838 supposedly the most-acculturated Indian group in the United States, were nevertheless Indians and subject to the same racist, discriminatory practices leveled at any Native American.

It is typical on a Saturday night at a Trail of Tears Singing to have between one thousand and two thousand people in attendance, this in a county whose total white and Indian population is less than seven thousand. The four-hundred-member Snowbird community is therefore usually outnumbered in turn by North Carolina Cherokees from the main reservation, Oklahoma Cherokees, local whites, and out-of-state whites. I can remember one Saturday night at a Trail of Tears Singing when the men of Zion Hill Baptist hauled every church pew outside to the singing ground. The clearing by Snowbird Creek was crammed with Indians and whites, men and women, young and old. The church pews bulged with people. Whites talked with Indians seated near them on the long pews, and efforts to appraise the singing groups encouraged Western and Eastern Cherokees and Indians and whites to chat. Several groups of people spread quilts or tablecloths on the ground and sat on these. In the warm summer weather the atmosphere was almost that of a carnival. Inside the community building food was busily being prepared, bought, and eaten to benefit the Trail of Tears Organization— food that included coffee, soft drinks, hot dogs, hamburgers, pastries, and a Cherokee specialty, bean bread. At the other end of the open ground, similar food items were being sold by members of the Snowbird Rescue Squad in their building to benefit their organization. Outside, all traffic control at the singing was in the hands of squad members. Over cups of coffee and pieces of bean bread, people from the diverse groups renewed old friendships or began new ones. The singing did not break up until well after midnight.

The white singing groups, whether local or from neighboring southern states, seemed more elaborately dressed than either the North Carolina or Oklahoma Cherokee groups. With few exceptions, women in white groups wore identical floor-length gowns, and the men almost always wore identical coats and ties. Occasionally the singers in a white group were not all dressed similarly, and occasionally this was also true of an Indian group. But even when the singers in an Indian group were all dressed alike, the women usually wore knee-length dresses, and the men seldom wore coats and ties. In one Oklahoma Cherokee quartet, for example, the two women wore green knee-length dresses, and the two men wore green shirts with black trousers but no coats or ties. An Oklahoma Cherokee trio was attired in identical red-checked dresses with white Indian vests with red fringe for the two women singers and white trousers and a red-checked shirt with red Indian fringe across the front and back for the man.

The most striking characteristic about the Indian singers, whether from Oklahoma or North Carolina, however, was not how they dressed but how they sang. Almost every Indian group sang some of its selections in the Cherokee language. The songs were standard gospel tunes, such as "Amazing Grace," but they were sung in Cherokee. Since the music was the same, even whites totally unfamiliar with the language knew the song being sung. In addition, in singing gospel songs in Cherokee the tonal quality of the spoken language disappears, and the Cherokee language is "Anglicized" and made to sound less foreign to those more accustomed to English. Many groups alternated languages, singing one verse of a song in English and then the same verse in Cherokee. Local whites, who do not speak any Cherokee but have become familiar with some of the lines of Cherokee versions of songs through repetition, would occasionally request a Cherokee version of a song by shouting out the first line in Cherokee to a group on stage. There was at least one North Carolina Cherokee group whose lead singer, a woman, does not speak the Cherokee language but has learned most of the Cherokee versions of popular songs through repeatedly hearing them sung. Many local whites think she speaks Cherokee.

The Snowbird Quartet is by far the most popular singing group from the Snowbird community. It is better organized than the informal groups who occasionally sing at the monthly Sunday church events. I have yet to attend a monthly church singing at which the Snowbird Quartet did not sing, and when they sing, they must fulfill many requests. Although the group has genuine singing talent plus the ability to use electric guitars and sound equipment, at first they do not appear as professional as other singing groups who invest in uniform stage clothes. I have never seen the group appear at an event, even the Trail of Tears Singing, dressed uniformly or wearing coats and ties. Nevertheless, the group is most popular and is invited to sing at neighboring white as well as Indian churches.

The present Snowbird Quartet is not the first Snowbird Quartet ever to be organized, and others will probably come later. The first one included the father of two of the present members. With one exception, members of the first group are dead. The Snowbird Quartet as a name and tradition is probably the oldest singing group in the Snowbird community. Despite shouts from the audience calling on the Snowbird Quartet to appear on stage, the group displayed traditional Indian modesty and performed last, after every guest group had performed. Perhaps because of the quartet's popularity, crowds remained at the Trail of Tears Singing until well after midnight when the Snowbird Quartet finally hit the stage singing "I'll Fly Away" in both English and Cherokee.

Both white churches and Indian churches have numerous singings throughout the year. Whichever group comprises the membership of the church acts as host, even if the guests vastly outnumber the church membership, which is often the case for Indian churches. At the Trail of Tears Singing, the entire Snowbird community, not just the organizers of the singing, was outnumbered by its guests. This condition was not resented but welcomed, since one of the main purposes of the singing was for Christians of any ethnic group to join together.

In a different context, the large turnout of Western Cherokees and people from other Eastern Cherokee communities reinforced Snowbird's image of itself as a real Indian community. In that sense, the Trail of Tears Singing is symbolic of the degree to which the community possesses crucial Cherokee traits and identifies as a Native American ethnic group. The 1838 removal over the Trail of Tears was a stark reminder to the Cherokees that no matter how acculturated they became they were still Indians. Otherwise they would never have been removed west. The modern Trail of Tears Singing likewise emphasizes the dual identity of a people involved in both acculturation and persistence.

The Trail of Tears Singing is, however, not only a vehicle for the expression of tribal and intertribal identity. It is also a major event for the voluntary association of local whites and Indians, for interethnic relations. For more than a century and a half, the land distribution pattern in the Graham County, North Carolina, area has meant Indians and whites have had intense, and usually harmonious, relations. Unlike the main reservation, the Qualla Boundary, where there are two large blocks of land, the thirteen small blocks of Snowbird reservation land are interspersed nearly checkerboard style with white-owned tracts. For more than a century, it has been virtually impossible for Snowbird Cherokees to live in isolation from non-Indians. Until the post–World War II tourist boom, many Cherokees on the main reservation were able to maintain such isolation. Because of its long history of relations with non-Indian communities, Snowbird is thus an appropriate location for an event like the Trail of Tears Singing that brings whites and Indians together. That Snowbird should bring together both Indian and white communities at a single event is symbolic of Snowbird's dual identity, with tribe and fellow Band members and with county and non-Indian neighbors.

Although the avowed purpose of the Trail of Tears Singing is religious, the event has other obvious aims. It is to a large extent also a social event that provides a scene for family reunions and the meeting of old friends, and an occasion for children to play and adults to eat out and be entertained by good music. The more casual dress of much of the crowd, the rambunctious play of the children, outbursts of applause and laughter, and little need to pay close attention to the events on stage all emphasize the purely social context of the event, in contrast to the more orderly monthly Sunday church singings.

For some, the Trail of Tears Singing also has an economic function. During the singing out-of-state white groups collect donations for the Trail of Tears Organization based at Zion Hill Baptist Church. Many of these same groups sell albums of their music at the singing and secure future bookings. Many local whites also benefit economically, since the influx of people increases business for grocery stores, cafes and restaurants, gasoline stations, and motels, all of which are owned and operated by whites.

If the singing reinforces common religious bonds between Indians and whites and benefits economically many whites, it also improves white-Indian relations to the advantage of Indians as well as whites. The common religious bonds that the two groups share may be expressed, but they are expressed in a uniquely Indian way, through the medium of the Cherokee language. Diversity and commonality are expressed in the same act of singing "Amazing Grace" in the Cherokee language.

Aside from the probable improvement of white-Indian relations, the event also functions to improve and maintain relations between Eastern and Western Cherokees. Although many people throughout the Eastern Cherokee reservation say that the Cherokee dialect spoken in Snowbird is closer than that of the main reservation to the dialect spoken in Oklahoma, there are still differences in the two versions of the Cherokee language. Snowbird Cherokees and Oklahoma Cherokees speak variations of the Atali dialect while Qualla Boundary Cherokees on the main reservation speak the Kituhwa dialect, often said by Eastern Cherokees themselves to be less pure and distinct than Atali. Because the Oklahoma version of Cherokee with which Eastern Cherokees are familiar is said to resemble Atali more than Kituhwa, it seems appropriate to have an intertribal event such as the Trail of Tears Singing at Snowbird, an Atali-speaking community. There are communication problems, however.

A Snowbird Cherokee organizer once described the dialect problems to me when he said, "We have a little trouble understanding each other. They got . . . a little different sound to their Indian language. Some of them you have to listen pretty close before you can understand it."

In 1974 when I asked Billy Fourkiller about language problems, he said, "We understand each other here in North Carolina. They talk a little bit different than we do, but it all still means the same deal, you know. . . . It's just a different pronunciation than we have because we got the real Cherokee language in Oklahoma. They said a long time ago when the Cherokees were driven from this area, they took the full-speaking Cherokees to Oklahoma. So the people here that hid out in the mountains, well, they just picked up what they could pick up of the language."

There are no political or legal ties joining North Carolina and Oklahoma Cherokees, and the federal government has officially viewed them as two distinct groups since 1886. They live too far away from each other—and have for more than a century and a half—to maintain any sort of intense relations, which is reflected by the differing dialects of Cherokee that they speak. They do, however, share a common language and a common religion. The two Cherokee groups also share a common respect for fullbloodedness and real Indianness, native craftsmen, practitioners of Indian medicine, and other symbols of Indian traditionalism. The Trail of Tears Singing symbolically reunifies the Cherokee people in their ancestral homeland. This major theme of the Trail of Tears Singing is manifested each time a Cherokee group, whether from

Oklahoma or North Carolina, takes the stage and begins to sing, as the Cherokees say, "in Indian." The event is a harmonious reuniting of the Cherokee Nation, especially those segments that view themselves as real Indians distinct from the wannabees and white Indians in their midst in both the west and east.

The Trail of Tears Singing in the Snowbird community is unique. One of the smallest of the Eastern Cherokee communities through one of its churches hosts the entire Cherokee Nation without the assistance of any other Cherokee community. One of the smallest Graham County communities hosts the rest of the county with no formal assistance from its non-Indian neighbors. In fact, whites from half a dozen states show up as guests of the Snowbird community. The event expresses the harmonious aspects of Snowbird's relations with other groups of people. Other Eastern Cherokees, Western Cherokees, and non-Indians all participate, but Snowbird is in charge.

Through the leadership of its churches, Snowbird Cherokee Indians have preserved their unique language, values, and identity for more than a century. For much of this century the monthly church singings have helped to improve white-Indian relations, and this has been intensified since 1968 with the large outdoor singings such as the older Trail of Tears Singing or more recent Billy Fourkiller Singing.

The original goal of white Christian missionaries may have been to change Cherokee culture. But as I reflected while attending the Billy Fourkiller Singing, in a community such as Snowbird the missionaries were only partially successful as the churches, firmly under Indian control, became institutions active in the preservation of traditional identity, language, and values.

NOTE

I wish to thank everyone in the Snowbird community, especially the Long and Jackson families, and the Eastern Band of Cherokee Indians as a whole for their help and support over the years.

Part 2

Conferred and Chosen Identities

Attacking (Southern) Creationists

Kary D. Smout

For more than a century, a heated debate has raged about whether creation or evolution should be taught in science classes in American public schools. This debate has led to what historian Ronald L. Numbers calls "some of the fiercest skirmishes in the annals of science and religion" (1992:xiv). To understand the fierceness and intractability of this controversy, I conducted an extended study of assumptions about language and strategies of persuasion used by both sides in several key episodes: the initial reception of Darwin's *Origin of Species,* the 1860 Huxley-Wilberforce debate at Oxford, the 1925 Scopes "Monkey" Trial, and the 1981 Arkansas Creation-Science Trial (Smout 1991). This essay focuses on one important pattern I discovered: some disturbing linkages forged by key evolutionists between creationism and southern fundamentalism.

This pattern was first developed in print by H. L. Mencken, the well-known journalist and writer of the 1920s. In his influential essay "The Sahara of the Bozart," Mencken launched a famous attack on the American South as a cultural desert free of any trappings of civilization, including literature, fine arts, or intellectual attainments (the "beaux arts" he parodied in his title). In a sentence near the beginning of his essay, Mencken introduces several key oppositions that he used extensively in his later attacks on creationism: "I say a [dried-up] civilization because that is what, in the old days, the South had, despite the Baptist and Methodist barbarism that reigns down there now" (1920:137). Here Mencken contrasts earlier southern civilization to current southern barbarism and links this barbarism to religion. He implies that the cultural decline of the South is linked to particular beliefs of Baptists and Methodists. What exactly do these barbaric religions block? "Obviously, it is impossible for intelligence to flourish in such an atmosphere.

59

Free inquiry is blocked by the idiotic certainties of ignorant men" (153). Mencken contends that the South has fallen to this level of stupidity because it lost its "superior men" in the Civil War: "The old aristocracy went down the red gullet of war; the poor white trash are now in the saddle" (139). Quoting another author, he describes some typical poor whites in Georgia as "the most degraded race of human beings claiming an Anglo-Saxon origin that can be found on the face of the earth—filthy, lazy, ignorant, brutal, proud, penniless savages" (147). Mencken's essay contains the seeds of a powerful negative representation of creationism. It suggests that idiotic religious beliefs are accepted only by ignorant southern white trash.

Five years later Mencken went to Dayton, Tennessee, to report on the best-known American battle between creation and evolution: the Scopes "Monkey" Trial. In this trial, John T. Scopes, a high school science teacher, was found guilty of violating a Tennessee law that forbade the teaching of evolution in public schools. Scopes was defended by the celebrated agnostic Clarence Darrow and prosecuted by three-time Democratic presidential candidate William Jennings Bryan, the foremost creationist of his day. Mencken covered the trial for all but the last day and actually coined its nickname "Monkey" in what have become his most-famous newspaper reports.

In these reports, Mencken fully develops a powerful negative representation of creationism that links it to southern fundamentalism. To set the scene for the trial, Mencken gives an interesting composite picture of Dayton. He writes in an early report: "I expected to find a squalid Southern town. . . . What I found was a country town full of charm and even beauty" (1965:36). But more widely known than this single genial depiction are repeated descriptions of Dayton as a fundamentalist haven, a "bright shining buckle of the Bible belt" (42), and reports about the Tennessee people who came from surrounding areas to watch the trial, swarming into Dayton to sell food and Bibles, wear sandwich boards proclaiming gospel slogans, attend prayer meetings, and otherwise make the trial resemble a carnival. Mencken's longest report— one posted on a bulletin board by the editor of the *Baltimore Evening Sun* as a paragon of reporting (Manchester 1983:177)—graphically narrates a pentecostal revival that Mencken attended in the mountains behind Dayton, complete with shouting in tongues, prayer circles, gifts of healing, physical contortions, and smells of heat and human sweat.

This report, published throughout the nation, painted a very unflattering picture of southern religion.

Throughout these reports, Mencken also attacks the creationists directly. He makes fun of "the so-called minds of these fundamentalists from upland Tennessee," ridiculing their "barbaric cosmogony" and "simian imbecility" (Mencken 1965:41, 45, 50). Turning to their leader, William Jennings Bryan, Mencken writes that Bryan perceived in a scientist called as an expert witness by Darrow "a sworn agent and attorney of the science he hates and fears—a well-fed, well-mannered spokesman of the knowledge he abominates" (46). Bryan is further depicted as a man of "peculiar imbecilities," "a tinpot pope in the Coca-Cola belt," and a dangerous "fanatic, rid of sense and devoid of conscience" under whose leadership "Neanderthal man is organizing in these forlorn backwaters of the land" (42, 48, 51). Mencken implies that the backwaters are the South, the Neanderthals the creationists, their leader a malicious fool who believes their barbaric religion, and the whole creationist movement an enemy of science, civilization, and learning as embodied in the theory of evolution.

The regional implications of Mencken's linkages did not go unnoticed. Many southerners were so upset that his periodical the *American Mercury* was banned for a time in small towns in the South (Fitzpatrick 1989:64). Mencken alienated not only rural people but also many southern writers, especially the Fugitive Poets of Nashville, who had originally rallied to his call in "The Sahara of the Bozart" for southern literature but now criticized his "complete dismissal of religious fundamentalism" and became "offended that [he] made their state the butt of national ridicule" (Hobson 1987:183). A leader of the Baltimore Chamber of Commerce even blamed Mencken's "unjust characterization of the people in the South" for a decline in southern business dealings with Baltimore (Manchester 1983:180).

When Bryan unexpectedly died a few days after the trial, Mencken attacked creationism and southern fundamentalism again in a piece that many critics consider his masterpiece. In his anti-eulogy for Bryan, "In Memoriam: W.J.B.," he dismisses creationism as a product of ignorant fundamentalist fanaticism and attacks creationists as subhumans. Mencken depicts the people of Tennessee who came to listen to the trial as "gaping primates from the upland valleys of the Cumberland Range," "people who sweated freely and were not debauched by the refinements of the toilet," men whose wives were "as fecund as the shad" (1926:65). He claims that Bryan was able to gather these Southern backwoodsmen because "he knew every country town in the South and the West, and he could crowd the most remote of them to suffocation by simply winding his horn"; "he was born with a roaring voice, and it had the trick of inflaming half-wits" (64, 68). Among many ad hominem attacks, Mencken compares Bryan to a dog with rabies, describes his "malicious animal magnetism" and his eyes that glittered "like occult and sinister gems," and asserts that Bryan was "deluded by a childish theology, full of an almost pathological hatred of all learning, all human dignity, all beauty, all fine and noble things" (68–71). Mencken concludes with a statement of gratitude that the nation was then governed by a boring Calvin Coolidge rather than by the "intolerable buffoonery" of a southern fundamentalist like Bryan. He writes: "We have escaped something—by a narrow margin. . . . That is, so far." Then he describes the remaining danger: "Heave an egg out of a Pullman window, and you will hit a Fundamentalist almost everywhere in the United States today. . . . They are everywhere where learning is too heavy a burden for mortal minds to carry, even the vague, pathetic learning on tap in little red schoolhouses" (73–74). Mencken depicts creationism not as a defensible intellectual position held by reasonable people but as a dangerous delusion linked to religious fundamentalism and political conservatism in uncivilized areas of the country such as the South. Although in the last quotation Mencken claims that fundamentalists are almost everywhere in the United States, his powerful descriptions of southern creationists and his carefully forged linkages between creationism, fundamentalism, barbarism, and ignorance effectively strengthened negative regional stereotypes in his own time. Mencken's descriptions may be the most vivid, but they are neither the first nor the last to suggest that the only people who believe in creationism are backward southerners more interested in rural politics and old-time religion than in the advance of scientific truth.

Mencken's negative representation of creationism was further disseminated and popularized by the 1955 play and 1960 film *Inherit the Wind,* a dramatized narration of the Scopes trial. Set in a rural town called Hillsboro notable for its oppressive heat, abundant preachers, and lack of cultural institutions except fundamentalist churches, this work clearly implies a setting in the South. It also includes a major character based on H. L. Mencken, whose writings about the Scopes trial are frequently quoted and paraphrased in the work. In the film version, the Mencken character is brilliantly played by Gene Kelly, the Bryan character by Fredric March, and the Darrow character by Spencer Tracy, but the story is mainly told from the viewpoint of a young woman who must choose between her creationist father, a fundamentalist preacher, and her evolutionist fiancé, the Scopes character. This young woman eventually leaves her father, rejecting his creationism and her fundamentalist upbringing in order to marry the agnostic biology teacher.

At one point, the film makes explicit its setting in the South. After a group of locals gather like a lynch mob to burn the Scopes character in effigy while he watches from a window above, they throw a bottle at him, breaking the glass and cutting his face. Within moments of this mock lynching, the Mencken character appears at the door wearing a white hood and says "boo." By including this potent symbol of the Ku Klux Klan, the film subtly suggests that southern creationists are also southern racists, that people who oppose evolution also burn blacks. This allusion would have had special impact in the early years of the civil rights movement immediately after the 1954 Supreme Court decision desegregating public schools.

The film implies a further attack on southern fundamentalism by shifting its theme song at the end from "Give Me That Old-Time Religion" to "The Battle Hymn of the Republic." After the protagonist has rejected creationism and fundamentalism in favor of the superior ideas of evolution and agnosticism, the film substitutes a hymn composed by an abolitionist during the Civil War for the fundamentalist hymn sung periodically throughout the rest of the work. This shift symbolically links creationism to the South and opposes both to evolution, the North, and God's truth that goes marching on.

Inherit the Wind thus introduced later generations of American viewers to Mencken's negative representation of creationism, effectively persuading them to link this position to southern fundamentalism. Among those directly influenced both by Mencken's writings and by this film is the nation's best-known contemporary critic of creationism, Harvard geologist and paleontologist Stephen Jay Gould. For more than a decade, Gould has written essays about the creation/evolution controversy and has attacked creationism in many forums, including public television programs. Just as Mencken was involved in the Scopes trial,

Gould served as an expert witness in the trial dubbed "Scopes II" by the media: the Arkansas Creation-Science trial of 1981. In this best-known recent confrontation between evolutionists and creationists, a state law was struck down as unconstitutional that required creationism to be taught in Arkansas public schools whenever evolutionism is taught. Although Gould has not to my knowledge ever attempted to ridicule the South directly in his attacks on creationism, he has continually represented creationism as an irrational idea accepted only by ignorant people who also happen to be political conservatives and religious fundamentalists.

While Gould was preparing for the trial in Little Rock, he visited the town of Dayton, Tennessee. In an essay on this visit—one of his earliest attacks on creationism—he reports that a Dayton minister recently "cited Darwin as a primary supporter of the four 'p's'—prostitution, perversion, pornography, and permissiveness"; after all, "they taught creationism in Dayton before John Scopes arrived, and they teach it today" (1983:269–70). Having identified creationism as an irrational religious belief, Gould then attacks Bryan as "a fundamentalist stumper—a 'tinpot pope in the Coca-Cola belt,' as H. L. Mencken remarked" and "a pompous fool" (265). Turning from Bryan to "our current creationist resurgence," Gould claims that contemporary creationists "debase religion even more than they misconstrue science" in their effort to "substitute biblical authority for free scientific inquiry as a source of empirical knowledge," thus contending that religious beliefs must not be confused with scientific knowledge (276). Later Gould writes: "We have nothing to fear" from the harmless fundamentalists who "live by a doctrine that is legitimately indigenous to their area. Rather, we must combat the few yahoos who exploit the fruits of poor education for ready cash and larger political ends" (278). By the end of this essay, Gould has indicated that if these yahoo-creationists (the contemporary counterpart for Mencken's white trash) are left unchecked, they may well create a scenario similar to Hitler's Germany. The essay thus represents creationism as an irrational position based on religious fundamentalism, accepted only by the ignorant, but used by the evil to launch a "movement of intolerance . . . that [could begin] in comedy, and [end], when successful, in carnage" (278). It is hard to imagine a more negative representation than one linking creationism to fundamentalism and comparing both to Hitler's Third Reich.

In his other essays on the controversy, Gould uses similar persuasive strategies to reject creationism as a product of irrational religious fundamentalism and to make ad hominem attacks on creationists. His essay "Moon, Mann, and Otto" starts by describing an editorial cartoon poking fun at Arkansas for "Scopes II" and ends by invoking God's blessings on those Arkansas teachers who reject creationism as "imposed antirationalism" and thus disprove common stereotypes about the South (1983:289). In "Genesis and Geology," Gould ridicules the central irrational belief of creationism/fundamentalism: "Biblical literalism will never go away, so long as cash flows and unreason retains its popularity" (1991:403). In "Evolution as Fact and Theory," he attacks creationists' motives: "Faced with these facts of evolution and the philosophical bankruptcy of their own position, creationists rely upon distortion and innuendo to buttress their rhetorical claim" (1983:259). In "Justice Scalia's Misunderstanding," he discusses the reprehensible tactics used by "fundamentalist groups" in "their recent aborted struggle to inject Genesis literalism into science classrooms," and he adds that "fundamentalism ranks among our most potent irrationalisms" (1991:455, 459). Recently, Gould has taken a break from these unremitting attacks on creationists as bad people and fundamentalism as an irrational religion by writing two sympathetic essays about William Jennings Bryan and Archbishop James Ussher (the man who placed the year of the creation as 4004 B.C. and gave a specific date and time) (1991; 1993). In these essays, Gould attempts to make sense of these two creationists from ages past, but to my knowledge he has not published a sentence about contemporary creationists that is not dripping with invective against them as individuals and dismissals of religious fundamentalism as the irrational core of creationism itself. Gould may link creationism to the South more tenuously than Mencken did, but he makes no less use of Mencken's two basic strategies in attacking southern creationists.

Although Mencken and Gould have done the most to advance this negative representation, two final examples will further illustrate this recurring linkage between creationism and southern fundamentalism. Another key witness at the Arkansas trial, Canadian historian and philosopher of science Michael Ruse, has written an essay about his experiences there in which he characterizes the position of the creationists as "a real intellectual and moral evil" defended by "sleazy" people plagued with "dishonest stupidity" (Ruse 1984: 322, 336). Ruse explains why creationism has been accepted at all: "In times of stress and unhappiness," fundamentalist religious beliefs appeal to people in the United States, "particularly in the South," who want "simplistic doctrines for support and comfort" (314). He concludes: "It is those who deny evolution who are anti-God, not those who affirm it" (334). In a less stereotypical but even more revealing statement, the judge in the Arkansas trial, William Overton, echoes similar sentiments in a talk he gave to Pennsylvania appellate judges at Bucknell University. Overton reports that the trial taught him not to think of a typical creationist as a "moonshiner in Eastern Tennessee" or "some Bible thumping preacher in a church down a dusty road in south Arkansas" but as a college-educated person who has roots in "the high technology soils of southern California" (1982:17). The outward appearance and occupation may change, but the region and religious affiliation remain the same. When even the judge in the Arkansas trial, himself a Methodist and a native Arkansan, reports that he expected creationists to be southern fundamentalist hillbillies and was surprised when they were only fundamentalists, one glimpses the cultural work done for decades by a single compelling representation.

How did I react when I first discovered this representation? Although I am neither a creationist, a fundamentalist, nor a southerner, I was disturbed by repeated efforts to depict creationists as irrational, uncivilized southern fundamentalists too stupid or too devious to accept an obvious truth. Is the truth of evolution obvious? If so, why can't the creationists see it? In an interview about creationism published in the *New York Times,* leading evolutionist Richard Dawkins says: "It is absolutely safe to say that if you meet someone who claims not to believe in evolution, that person is ignorant, stupid, or insane (or wicked, but I'd rather not consider that)" (1989:35). I think our society can find better ways to argue this controversy than following Mencken, Gould, and Dawkins in implicitly or explicitly labeling those with whom they disagree as ignorant, stupid, wicked, or insane. Participants from both sides need to understand how their opponents see the world rather than just accusing each other of blindness. They need to get beyond regional, religious, and other stereotypes to forge a common language, to discover common ground from which to argue if they want to resolve the controversy through mutual persuasion.

Constructing Christian Hatred: Anti-Catholicism, Diversity, and Identity in Southern Religious Life

Gary W. McDonogh

In his 1992 New Year's Eve homily, a white Georgia Roman Catholic priest reminded his predominantly black congregation: "You know there are people who don't think Catholics are Christians. . . . They are very prevalent in the South . . . even in our city, Oh yes. Because we don't act out the part. We need to show them we are Christians. That we are even more so because of the sacraments, our belief in the Real Presence." This passage epitomizes three primary features of anti-Catholicism in southern religious life that this essay considers: presence, response, and division. This discussion first focuses on those in the South who have defined their Christianity by rejection of others. Whether realized in evangelical debates with Rome, the politics of nativism, or myths of the Vatican as apocalyptic symbol, anti-Catholicism evokes multiple origins, expressions, and social meanings. Even while the rhetoric of most contemporary Christian denominations eschews past vivid images, residues of bigotry remain in doctrinal confessions, social institutions, and memories.

This essay also explores the sermon's call to witness, which underscores the extent to which southern Catholics have responded to prejudice in their own identities. Their incorporation permeates institutions, political blocs, and beliefs that I have documented in modern Savannah (McDonogh 1987, 1993; see McNally 1987; Anderson 1992). Both Catholics and Protestants have reified "the Catholic as Other," holding dialectical readings of a divisive myth.

The sermon's context, a predominantly black parish, indicates a final element of this analysis. Much of the literature of anti-Catholicism—and, indeed, of southern religion—builds on the biracial divide of black and white within which Catholics have been identified with ethnic Euro-Americans. However, Catholics of color in the South, including older black congregations and newer Hispanic and Asian populations, often have found themselves in opposition to white Catholics as well as to white non-Catholics. This shapes distinctive experiences of Christian hatred among Catholics of color, and yet transforms these into multi-cultural theologies of community, identity, and belief.

This essay grows from both academic research on Catholicism in the South since 1982 and personal experience over several decades more concerning southern and Catholic experiences. Although my primary fieldwork focused on the contradictions of black and Catholic identity in Savannah, it was motivated, in part, by my Irish-American Catholic heritage in Kentucky and my perceptions of culturally constructed conflicts between "southernism" and Catholicism. Thus, I have collected anti-Catholic materials as both an academic and a reflexive exercise throughout the South while placing them in historical and social contexts, including long-term conversations with Protestant and other friends. This discussion begins to organize these materials, then, according to the tripartite scheme that I have set forth.

HATING CATHOLICS: SOCIAL ACTION
AND SYMBOLIC INTERPRETATION

Anti-Catholicism imbued the religious foundations of the American colonies and their heritages in the new Republic. The first European Catholic migrants to the United States thus faced nativist suspicion and urban riots: "*Irish* and *Catholic* also meant enemy to many Protestant Americans" (Ochs 1990:17). Only later did the growing political clout and socioeconomic mobility of immigrant enclaves of the North and Midwest challenge this prejudice effectively; even so, prejudice lingered quietly in many circles, while some Northern European Catholics reproduced nativist imagery in disdain toward later Southern and Eastern European arrivals (Greeley 1977; Orsi 1985). Within this evolution, however, the South became set apart by the perdurance and renewal of anti-Catholicism and the lack of active Catholic population, outside of a few cities, to oppose it (Miller and Wakelyn 1983; McNally 1987).

Georgia populist Tom Watson (1856–1922) understood the political value of anti-Catholicism. Watson had originally built his career on appeals to a common man in opposition to the rich. Yet after setbacks in the early 1900s, such works as *Roman Catholics in America Falsifying History and Poisoning the Minds of Schoolchildren* (1917) solidified his audience around other prejudices: "Frustrated in their age-long, and eternally losing struggle against a hostile industrial economy, the farmers, together with a large depressed urban element, welcomed exciting crusades against more vulnerable antagonists: against anything strange, and therefore evil. Vicarious as were such easy victories, they offered some tangible compensations to a people hungry for satisfactions" (Woodward 1938:418–19). Indeed, Watson discriminatingly combined Catholics, blacks, and Jews as "Others." Thus, after he incited Leo Frank's 1915 lynching through bitter anti-Semitism, he railed that if lynching did not mean that "THE VOICE OF THE PEOPLE IS THE VOICE OF GOD . . . let us abandon our Republican form of Government, kiss the Pope's foot, and ask him to appoint a 'divine right' king to rule over us" (Woodward 1938:445).

This apogee of public anti-Catholicism faded after the new Klan's heyday in the 1920s, diminished by regional educational and economic development. Yet suspicions rekindled with the John F. Kennedy presidential campaign of 1960. Before an audience of Houston ministers, for example, Kennedy seemed compelled to relegate Roman Catholicism to a political nonissue, all the while evoking the specter of political martyrdom by religious intolerance. This ultimately proved strategic in both the North and South (see White 1961:237–43, 260–62, 390–93).

Subsequent demographic shifts in the Sunbelt South have, in fact, produced a larger population of Catholic immigrants from the North and Midwest as well as from foreign parishes. In this ambience, many Protestants I interviewed in Savannah denied any prejudice among their co-religionists—or imputed it to a more backward, rural, or illiterate version of southern evangelicalism. A Presbyterian friend from Kentucky summarized his feelings by converting anti-Catholicism to a distant relic: "We heard about it in Sunday School. About the reasons in the past for the division of the churches. But anti-Catholicism was something in the past, to be ashamed of." While public appeals to anti-Catholicism have become less acceptable, post–Vatican II Catholics are more openly critical of official church positions diffusing critical discourse. Nonetheless, sporadic outbursts, memories, and documents betray the ongoing transformative power of inherited myths (Sahlins 1981) that have embedded anti-Catholicism in southern religion. These are complicated by the diverse metaphoric networks that constitute anti-Catholic expression, drawing on historical images as well as vague archetypes. Vivid but disparate symbols mingle church history, demonic power, competition, and ignorance in a heady emulsion that theologian James Thompson has recalled from his Adventist childhood in Maryland and Washington, D.C.:

> Reduced to its essentials it amounted to this: the Pope would league with Satan and the Communists to persecute God's remnant. Our preachers did not view the Roman Church in prosaic institutional terms; they transformed it into the "Scarlet Woman," the "Whore of Babylon" and a dozen other scintillating and often sexual metaphors that captivated me. . . . Although I had never ventured inside a Catholic church (the mere thought of which made my skin crawl) my imagination compensated for the absence of experience. Yes, I knew what went on behind those walls: acrid incense choked the air; flickering candles cast phantasmagorical shadows; priests mumbled incantations in a garbled and hideous tongue; statues scarcely different from pagan idols lined the walls; black boxes lurked in darkened recesses; and those benighted Catholics—victims of their own gullibility—prostrated themselves before garishly decorated altars. . . . It was all terribly frightening to a Protestant country boy—and, somewhere deep within his subconscious, fascinating and alluring as well. (1986:49–50)

In reading the speeches, accusations, or documents of diverse anti-Catholic sources, I am struck constantly by the transcendent detachment of motifs that sometimes antedate the Reformation, made seemingly incontrovertible by their very diffuseness and disparities. Generally, the imagery of anti-Catholicism draws on one or more of these metaphoric clusters: (1) the "Whore of Babylon/Sins of the Apocalyptic Church" complex, which identifies Catholicism as a symbol of absolute and diabolic evil, at times in conjunction with other secular evils such as communism, Stalin, or Hitler (see Chiniquy 1886; Chick comics 1982, n.d.); (2) the "Fallen Church," whose erroneous doctrine and practice underpinned Reformation debates, ranging from transubstantiation to the meaning and power of the confessional (Chiniquy 1886; Chick n.d.); (3) the "Power-mad Papacy/Clergy" charges, which focus attention on ecclesiastical hierarchy—popes, bishops, priests, and sometimes nuns—as both religious and secular forces (Watson 1917); or (4) the "Submissive Foreign Flocks" motif, which humanizes and ethnicizes attacks on Catholics as a civil community of immigrants, victims of their clergy but potential competitors in economic and political arenas.

In practice, the use of these elements as rhetorical tropes and calls to action takes many forms. Through the period of my work in Savannah since 1981, for example, sporadic unclaimed posters identified the pope, *Time* magazine, and the KGB as lurking enemies within yet another definition of America (Thompson 1986:131 cites the same posters). Here Catholicism as signifier confirms the presence of absolute evil. While distant from Know-Nothing riots or Watsonian harangues, as Sahlins notes, "the historical process unfolds as a continuous and reciprocal movement between the practice of the structure and the structure of the practice" (1981:72). Yet this multiform prejudice is also reified—and perhaps maintained—by Catholic memory, institutional and popular.

ANTI-CATHOLICISM AND EURO-SOUTHERN CATHOLIC IDENTITY

Early issues of the *Bulletin of the Catholic Layman's Association of Georgia* from the 1920s evoke different perspectives on anti-Catholicism. The association, founded by Richard Reid to combat Watson and other critics (Cashin 1962), featured headlines ranging from personal responses—"Ex-Nun's State Tour a Failure: Small Audiences Except in Macon, Where She Was Refused Municipal Auditorium" (25 January 1922:7)—to more specific counteraccusations—"Savannah Grand Jury Finds 'Scant Warrant' for Convent Inspection" (15 December 1922:15), "Knights of Columbus Offer $5000 Reward in Georgia for Proof They Take Notorious Alleged Oath" (15 May 1923), and significantly, "Why Catholics Are Feared" (23 February 1924). Thus the apologetic press reinforced vivid myths of anti-Catholic traditions while turning them into a crusade for pride and presence among Georgia Catholics.

Other interpretations of Catholic superiority through social martyrdom in the South permeate local Catholic historiography. Father Jeremiah O'Connell's 1879 reports on anti-Catholic attacks and convent burnings during the Civil War burning of Columbia, South Carolina, for example, interpreted this event by identification of heroic Catholics and unruly Protestants with biblical forebears: "the guard resembled in temper the men who led St. Ignatius from Antioch to Rome to be devoured by wild beasts for the amusement of the cultivated citizens of the metropolis. History repeats itself; and with few modifications men are always and everywhere the same, whether in Rome under Nero, in Paris under Robespierre, or in Columbia" (281).

Traces of similar interpretations have remained alive to older Euro-American Catholics with whom I have worked in Savannah. Their vast corpus of folklore mingled experiences, reports, and feelings that had shaped their lives as Catholics, unifying anti-Catholicism as myth and praxis into their own cultural worldview. One educated man in his eighties, for example, recalled his father's stories of the visit of a so-called former priest to Savannah nearly a century before (1893). He added stories from friends and pastors as well as his own life: "Watson was a bad man—have you read his articles in the *Mentor?* Yet he wrote a definitive history of France and has a statue in the capitol. . . . But he sent his two daughters to Catholic schools and used to talk to Bishop Keiley on the train on the way up. Still, I remember one he wrote: that bones were found at St. Vincent's and that there was a tunnel connecting St. Vincent's Academy and the Cathedral. Terrible." Here historical memory confirms a beleaguered Catholic presence while showing Watson as a hypocrite and mythmonger. Another professional directed me to the Vesey Bill, which mandated inspections of convents for suspicions of white slavery. He recalled this bill through his memories of serving on grand juries charged to consider such myths.

Still other tales turned anti-Catholic rhetoric into indictments of rural Protestant ignorance. One anecdote told about a local Catholic bishop, "visiting a small town when a man said, 'Father, would you mind doing something for me even though I am not Catholic?' 'Yes,' he said. 'Would you take off your shoes and socks?' See, he wanted to see if he had cloven hooves. And the Bishop did!" The story simultaneously exalts the bishop's wisdom and tolerance while denigrating his interrogator. The same wry manipulation informs the observations of Georgia Catholic author Flannery O'Connor (1979). Such narratives define Catholics by inverting anti-Catholic myths so as to reject southern Protestants and their cultural hegemony.

These memories also point to complexities of southern Catholic society and culture. Historical frameworks underpin divergent interpretation of events, past and future. As I noted in an earlier article, urban ethnic and class narratives of history and identity differed in their appropriation of anti-Catholicism (McDonogh 1987). Thus Irish-Americans who have dominated Savannah's Catholic population over the past century recalled an aggressive antagonism in the 1920s as well as a tumultuous era of integration and Catholic changes with Vatican II in the 1960s. Italians and Germans, by contrast, conflated religious persecution with ethnic tensions arising from the world wars while Cajuns, settled at a nearby sugar refinery, faced everyday tensions in the evangelical countryside.

Anti-Catholicism also affirmed an urbane identity for Roman Catholic Savannahians. Although rural Catholic communities experienced isolation and intense debate (Anderson 1992), a Savannah businessman born at the turn of the century interpreted a rural experience very differently: "About Al Smith's time, this tire dealer in a small town said, 'You're from Savannah?' 'Yes.' 'How 'bout these Catholics? Aren't they terrible?' I thought about it and said, 'You may not like me but I'm a Catholic' (thinking, there goes the sale!) But you know, he liked me better."

Class has shaped still other divisions whose repercussions in the interpretation of anti-Catholicism prove complex. In Savannah, status and gender seem to be mutually dependent in narratives. Thus more than one upwardly mobile Catholic woman complained about a glass ceiling that excluded Catholics from social events or from elite societies such as the Colonial Dames. Males were less concerned with these than with political and economic power, public factional competition between neighborhoods, and schools and parties rather than individual or family evaluation. To another working-class Irishman, however, even recognition of elite problems represented treason to Catholic society, part of a stereotypic "female vanity": "There are some Irish who try to become 'social,' but others turn their back on them. And they never make it to first base and they become snobs. But they want to make it into the Oglethorpe club and have their daughters debutantes" (age 79, interviewed on 8 July 1982).[1]

Historiography, memory, and the interpretation of experience thus sustain identities among southern Catholics that have incorporated the prejudice of their neighbors as well as their own triumph as communities and individuals. While grappling with diversity, a shared belief in the external reality of hatred has evoked a consciousness of unity. As Father Clyde Crews prefaces his history of the Louisville Catholic archdiocese: "If Faulkner was right that the past is never really *past,* he couldn't be more right about it than in the case of Kentucky Catholicism. History lives here as a presence, both brooding and benevolent" (1987:25–26). Yet both Catholic and Protestant experience in the South also has been fundamentally divided by the cultural construction of race.

COLOR, CLASS, AND SECTARIANISM:
ALTERNATIVE PERSPECTIVES

"Suspected of Preaching Catholic Doctrine, Negro Minister Beaten," screamed another headline from the early Georgia Catholics' *Bulletin* (25 March 1922:10). "Your damned bishop came here preaching Catholicism and got away before we could get him. Then he sent you here with your Catholic doctrine, educating these damned negroes and making them worse." Another report highlighted minister Joe Harker, who decried an army of one million Catholics ready to attack on the pope's orders. It cited Harker's claims that "Catholics are trying to convert the negro to their faith on the promise that they will be put on an equality with the white man," charges that appealed "in one breath to the religious and racial prejudice of his audience" (*Bulletin* 25 April 1922:5). In both stories, Catholics are portrayed as Euro-American outsiders who wish to manipulate blacks for their own ends. The "Catholic" response, in turn, denies Euro-American responsibility rather than appealing to African American actions or voices. The newspaper's defense implies that Catholics (meaning white Catholics) would never believe blacks to be equal; indeed, it construes the charge itself as anti-Catholic. This attitude underlies claims by some black Catholics that they are marginalized in the decision making and even the worldview of the Catholic church (Griffin 1979; McDonogh 1993).

Given these experiences and the questions they raise, black perspectives on anti-Catholicism differ from those of southern white Catholics. Religion, for example, proved an ambivalent marker of public identity in interracial settings: as one older black and Catholic Savannahian remarked to me in 1982, "the Klan didn't care if you were Catholic, if you were Black." Nor did the Irish immigrants who constituted the backbone of the nineteenth-century church seem in any way natural class allies of African Americans, so much as alien competitors privileged by the color of their skin (Levine 1977). The racism that painfully divided southern Catholicism eclipsed religious communion completely when blacks faced a more generally white and prejudiced society. Although white missionary priests and nuns—often foreign— might become legends in black communities, there could be no expectation of similar generosity of spirit from southern Catholic laity or even their clergy. In fact, in Savannah, such religious are often identified by blacks as "our" sisters or "just like one of us." These extensions of race are confirmed by memories that other Catholics (including clergy) would refer to such missionaries as "nigger sisters/priests."

Tensions between black Protestants and Catholics, however, did not reproduce Euro-southern models. Black Protestants have argued doctrinal differences, liturgical pomp, white domination, and emotional coldness against Catholicism, as black Catholics have responded with characterizations of evangelicals and Pentecostals by rural illiteracy or uncontrolled piety. Yet these differences, as I have observed in Savannah, are tempered by an intimacy of connections absent among whites. Many black Catholics are converts with memories and kindred among Protestants. Meanwhile, many modern black Protestants were exposed to Catholic missionary schools and neighborhood efforts.

I have argued at length that the points of difference between those who are black and Catholic and those who are either black and Protestant or white and Catholic have combined to create strong communities of survival. Yet any probing of the role of anti-Catholicism in black communities reveals the suspicions of racism from southern Euro-Catholics that also underpins black and Catholic parish and collective identity (McDonogh 1993). A failure to perceive these historical differences provides a metaphoric framework for continued division. Hence the bishop's seemingly liberal decision to integrate Savannah Catholic schools in the 1960s by closing black parishes became a gesture of martyred spirituality among white congregations who perceived change as their enemy, while it was read as a gesture of deaf paternalism by blacks inside the same church (Griffin 1979; McDonogh 1993). Thus even as the thrust of the past two decades in the southern Catholic church has been toward a unifying consciousness, the heritage of past racism means that many constructed hatreds continue to be projected into the future.

The responses of newer immigrant Catholics of color in the South demand spaces that reshape these combinations of sentiment and identity. Many Hispanic immigrants, for example, have arrived with knowledge of transnational struggles that pit a variety of non-Catholic churches against Roman Catholicism as a traditional religion throughout Latin America. Here, as in the case of blacks in the southern church, criticisms by laity and immigrants have inspired reforms. Nonetheless these often have failed to deal with class as well as language and ethnicity. My limited exposure to Hispanic, East Asian, and Southeast Asian Catholic communities in the South suggests that while elements of anti-Catholicism may shape their world, these are complicated by real problems ranging from paternalism to a kind of secondhand access to churches with which predominantly white parishes have met new migrant groups. At the same time, crises arise from tensions of language, ethnicity, and immigrant status that divide the urban and national context of any shared religion.

The experience of anti-Catholicism in communities of color in the South, then, differs from that of many Euro-American Catholics even as it evokes many of the same central symbolic expressions. These differences reveal the continuous interlocking of social, historical, and cultural features in southern religion and identity, as well as the depths of the wounds that continue to sunder the publicly Christian South.

Significant nuances for southern religious life emerge in probing myth and strategies that spring from the social dialectic defined by anti-Catholicism. Among Protestants, in fact, there exist more divisions with regard to class, education, urbanity, race, and gender than I have elaborated. To incorporate these into a social topography of hatred, we must explore further correspondences among rhetoric, liturgy, preaching, and belief that link these divisions to images and social interplay with Catholics as well as to a genealogical investigation of myth and action. When an anti-Catholic comic based on a nineteenth-century Quebecois text repeating medieval myths is produced in California, sold in the Southeast, and left on the windshield of a priest on Tybee Beach, we must question the commercial commodification of hatred and the range of understandings of both historical metaphor and its concrete manifestations that this chain embodies (Chiniquy 1886; Chick 1982; see McDonogh 1993).

In further assessments of this dialectic of bigotry and identity, we might also note traditions of Catholic anti-Protestantism. In older catechism, for example, doctrinal differences become manifest as a lack of salvation "outside the True Church." These are echoed by a rich folklore of stories about Baptists, Episcopalians, and "Holy Rollers." Above all, these become manifest in separations of belief and ritual between Catholic and Protestant worlds. Yet disparities of power shape myths and practices. Dominant Protestants imposed themselves as unmarked and "normal"; southern Catholics adapted, resisted, or transcended this civic religion but could not reinvent it.

Catholic appropriation of southern prejudice also suggests other processes of division. The appeal to martyrdom as a self-identity also established contrasts between the southern Catholic missionary church and the North/Midwest as a richer Catholic heartland. The Catholic appeal to universalism, embodied in missions to blacks as well as in more recent support for Hispanics and Asians, must face a nativism that has established itself within southern Catholic congregations.

These explanations, however, return us to the central need for more exploration of the complexities of hatred itself in southern religion. In his unique early study of anti-Catholicism in American life, Andrew Greeley argued that it posed a more generally compelling problem for research because of its lack of recognition *per se:* "Good American liberals who would not dream of using sexist language or racist slurs or anti-Semitic jokes have no problems at all about using anti-Catholic language, ethnic slurs, or Polish jokes. They are not hypocrites or fakers or self-conscious anti-Catholics; they are simply unaware of the nativist strains that run through their personalities and the nativist bias in the way they look at the world and describe it" (1977:1). My explorations of the social and cultural constructions of anti-Catholicism in the South suggest that Greeley, in fact, viewed the problem from a vastly different regional understanding that tends to typify Catholic social studies in the United States. In the South for most of its history, anti-Catholicism hardly has been secret, nor nativism sinful. Protestants and Catholics, whites and blacks, natives and immigrants have recognized anti-Catholicism as a socially constructed fact of life and built identities around it even as they may have contested (or used) it. To understand the religious mosaic of the South, then, we must ask about hate as well as love.

NOTES

Support for this research has been provided by New College and the University of South Florida as well as the Bible Belt Catholics Project of the Catholic University of America. Comments on this draft have been given by Cindy Hing-Yuk Wong and Jon Anderson as well as others who remain anonymous.

1. Discussions of class and power also pervade the differences of ordained leaders and laity. This may prove to be another area of potential confluence, however, between Protestant and internal Catholic critiques (McDonogh 1993).

Stranger in a Strange Land:
The Non-Christian as Alien in the South

Brenda G. Stewart

"I don't think the Unitarian denomination addressed the issue of being in an alien environment." When, in the course of the first interview I conducted, I heard this statement, I did not need to ask what was meant by "alien environment." As a long-time member of the Unitarian Universalist Fellowship of Winston-Salem, I knew. To Unitarian Universalists, the South is alien, even—perhaps especially—to those of us who grew up here. This alienation occurs along three major dimensions: religion, politics, and, to a lesser degree, education. We are surrounded by conservative and/or fundamentalist Christians, political conservatives, and anti-intellectuals. Only later did I realize that this explicit self-identification as alien would provide a clue to some of the paradoxes and contradictions that had bedeviled my research. This research, in fact, stemmed from a paradox: on the home turf of fundamentalist Christianity, a liberal denomination is growing rapidly. I now think there is a simple and straightforward explanation for this growth, namely demographic changes in the area. Nevertheless, in framing the issues as a research question, I found I had to consider such fundamental questions as: Does a religious institution have to be based on religion? What is religion? Is a group what its members say it is? How does that identity develop? I will address briefly how these questions underlie the paradox stated in the title of a recent Unitarian Universalist guide, "a religion for the non-religious" (Bartlett and Bartlett 1990).

Religion, defined by *Webster's Collegiate* as "the service and worship of God or the supernatural," is commonly understood and for most American religious institutions, especially Christian churches, is explicitly claimed to be a church's raison d'être. Although there is disagreement, such theorists as Stark and Bainbridge (1985:3–5) restrict the term to those systems based on a belief in the supernatural. Unitarian Universalism, however, does not require that its members profess belief in any form of divinity. Nationally and locally, 20 percent consider even the concept of God irrelevant or harmful and only 4 percent accept the concept of a supernatural God (Commission 1989:34; Dawson 1991:9). Yet in form and self-attribution, Unitarian Universalism is a religion. Similar rites, rituals, and organizational structure are found in various Christian denominations, and that national arbiter, the Internal Revenue Service, has confirmed its status. Clearly, part of the contradictions stems from the nature of the definition: the former, with its insistence on belief in the supernatural, is ideological; the latter is functional. Rather than argue that one or the other is the correct definition, I shall use "religious institution" when speaking of function and "religion" or "religious" in the narrow sense of Stark and Bainbridge. The question then becomes what functions of religion are being served when nonreligious people appropriate religious rituals and organizational structures? The dimensions of alienation revealed in the interviews I conducted provide some answers.

Alienation, of course, has its own particular definitions, especially in Marxist and legal discourse. However, I know of no better word to describe a feeling of being separate and/or different from those with whom one associates. Alienation in this sense is problematic for humans as social beings, and various strategies may be used to lessen or eliminate it. Those who experience this alienation because they reject religion achieve at least a superficial commonality with their Christian neighbors by affiliation with a religious institution—they too have a place to go on Sunday morning.

Narrative, in various forms, provides the data for my research. Story telling is an intrinsic part of interaction in Unitarian Universalist congregations, used quite self-consciously and with intent, as stories are "tools for understanding and negotiating reality" (Wesley 1987:10). I have drawn on several sources, including my own experience, for these stories. In an attempt to simulate one typical form, I begin my interviews with the question, "Where did you begin, religiously speaking, and what path led you from there to the denomination and the Fellowship?" This is intended to elicit what is known in the denomination as a spiritual journey narrative, a device commonly used in any inter- or intracongregational meeting other than a Sunday service. The narrative serves as an icebreaker and to integrate newcomers into the group.

Another form in which stories are found is the written record. *New Dimensions of the Spirit,* compiled by a long-term member and printed in 1982, "is the story of the Unitarian Universalists of Winston-Salem, North Carolina, as remembered by its members and documented in its records" (Zimmerman 1982:iii). It includes corporate myths as well as individual reminiscences. A third narrative source is a congregational meeting during "Start-Up Weekend" preceding the official installation of the new minister. The district executive conducting the meeting asked the group to construct a timeline, a history of the congregation as it was remembered. The group was told not to worry about the facts, that the memories were what was important. After construction of the timeline, the group was asked to describe itself, based on the incidents recorded. The self-description compiled on this specific occasion is not notably different from the one that appears in the interviews I conducted, and the seeds of it are found in the written story. From all sources, desire for fellowship and community is clear, as is rejection of the supernatural, particularly in the form associated with conservative Christianity.

The picture that emerged from "Start-Up Weekend" was of a strong, caring community, explicitly non-Christian, politically liberal, and with a "fortress mentality." It could have been equally drawn from the story recorded in *New Dimensions of the Spirit.* The following passage quotes an early member, a "displaced person" and transplanted Yankee who "found the parochialism and pervasive fundamentalism distressing": "We bit our tongues all week in the local stores, banks, offices, and neighborhoods; but, oh, on Sunday night we could SAY WHAT WE THOUGHT . . . even if next week we thought differently" (Zimmerman 1982:13–14).

The importance of community and fellowship permeated the interviews as well. It showed up in the spiritual journey narratives and in response to questions about the relative importance of Unitarian Universalist and non–Unitarian Universalist friends. One long-time member was asked: "How would you describe your level of involvement with the Fellowship?" She replied, "My second home and family—maybe it's my first family." A member who joined in the seventies said: "I really value the friendships I have there and just feel that it's a really caring family community. And if I had a need it would certainly be met, quickly, instantly, unconditionally."

The third element emerging from memories, the "fortress mentality," actually encompasses both non-Christian and politically liberal characteristics and places these in opposition to the South. This showed up clearly in interviews, starting with the member who said she and her family joined "in defense against the alien environment." Southern and Christian were frequently equated by nonsoutherners and southerners; most negative comments about the South assumed this equation. As one put it, "I want to go here [the Fellowship] because the Baptists get after you when you move." Another "was shocked [that] people would come to the door asking us to join their church." Over half of those interviewed made negative remarks about Christianity, especially conservative or fundamentalist Christianity. This negativity is spread evenly across the range of joining dates. The one remaining charter member said, "I'm angry at Christianity. I think we'd have a cure for cancer right now if it hadn't been for the Catholic Church in Europe in the Dark Ages." A member who joined in the sixties said, "That word to me sometimes has a kind of a negative connotation. I'm not sure I want to be called a Christian." Only three identify themselves as Christians unequivocally, while two more consider themselves Christians in some sense.

Five anti-southern remarks were noted that did not specifically refer to the Christian aspect of southern identity. These referred to the political conservatism of the area, particularly racist or anti–civil rights attitudes.

Political liberalism, the second aspect of "fortress mentality," in a city and state that are predominantly conservative, is the norm for this group. Of forty-one interviewees, thirty-six identified themselves as Democrats, with another "more liberal than the Democrats." One of three Republicans described himself as "an economic conservative and a social liberal." Another said, "I'm liberal. Very. . . . I have an open mind and I judge by results, [but] I've almost always been a Republican."

Another contrast between this group and the larger community is the uncommonly high level of education. McWhiney (1988:193) notes that "Most Southerners . . . had far less regard for formal education than did the average Northerner," and in the county in which Winston-Salem is located 23 percent have less than a high school education while only 24 percent have completed four or more years of college (Bureau of the Census 1990:51). This is quite different from those interviewed: all have some education beyond high school; 92 percent have a four-year degree or more; 27 percent have an M.D., a Ph.D., or one of those plus another advanced degree.

Finally, most members do not have local family or childhood ties that may transcend differences in views. Zimmerman notes (1982:4) that only four of the eleven charter members were from the city. Only two of those interviewed are locals and southerners as a whole are a minority, although the percentage is increasing. Three who are technically considered southerners, having grown up in Virginia, implicitly disassociate themselves: "We were only beginning to adapt to the Southern culture, having come from the Washington, D.C., area."

As mentioned earlier, one reason people give for joining the Winston-Salem Fellowship is that they can tell their Christian neighbors they belong to a church. Stump provides support for this idea when he states that "migrants to regions where cultural norms support higher levels of commitment, such as the South for white Protestants, tend to shift toward those higher levels" of religious commitment (1984:302). Socioeconomic factors reinforce this: "increase[d] religious participation [is especially likely] among persons of higher status in the South, where the church is the dominant social organization" (Stump 1986: 216). If a nonreligious person is going to affiliate with a religious institution, Unitarian Universalism is a logical choice. Unitarianism and Universalism emerged separately from within the Christian tradition and formally joined institutional structures in 1961. The association has clearly evolved from its Christian origins into a non-Christian ideology. According to a nationwide survey in 1967, 43 percent classified themselves as Christians; by 1987 that figure had dropped to 20 percent (Commission 1989:32).

Thus institutionally, Unitarian Universalism is a congenial environment for those who are actively non-Christian. Yet, it retains an organizational structure and rituals similar to those of mainstream Christian denominations. The extent to which these resemble their Christian counterparts varies between congregations and within any one congregation over time. Vygotsky, as discussed in Holland and Valsiner

(1988:261), provides support for the use of religious forms by those
nonreligious persons who have rejected a previous commitment to religion: "Objects and behaviors that have served in the past as mediating
devices are likely to continue to evoke the models or general understandings associated with the devices regardless of present goals." The mediating devices—tools or symbols "with which they arrange and organize
their mental worlds" (248)—in this case are the organizational structure
and types of behavior. Many goals are held in common with members of
Christian churches. Unitarian Universalists as well as Christians desire
to understand the world in which we live, to cooperate with and improve
the lot of our fellow humans, even though there may be radical disagreement on how and why this is to be done. From this perspective, one
would expect that specific behaviors and organizational characteristics
which evoke understandings associated with retained goals or with goals
held in common with those from other denominations are likely to be
incorporated into the current repertoire, those associated with rejected
goals, to be rejected. But since membership in the group is continually
changing and members do not necessarily share associations, there is
also a continual dialectic, negotiating and renegotiating exactly what is
and is not to be included and how it is to be interpreted.

As expected, support for those elements promoting social goals is
strong. The coffee hour, social activities at times other than Sunday
morning, and participatory elements of the Sunday morning program
are frequently mentioned as reasons for attending services.

Anything evoking religion or the authoritarianism and dogmatism at-
tributed to Christianity is likely to be contested. The very name, the
Unitarian Universalist Fellowship, is one of those contested areas. For
many years members of this local group resisted even using the term
"church" in reference to their Fellowship, and most are still adamant
that the name is not to change, although they may well speak of their
"church." Clerical authority is resisted as well. In contrast to most
other denominations and to older Unitarian Universalist churches, this
group was lay-led for much of its history, and there was a strong, vocal
contingent who objected to the decision to hire a permanent minister.
Ministerial contracts explicitly outline the duties of the minister and
the authority reserved for the Board of Trustees. Not until 1987, at the
instigation of the newly called minister, was instituted the practice of

having a standard format for Sunday programs; even then the minister was expected to speak no more than twice a month.

Finally, the most hotly contested program-related issue of recent years has been the "talkback." This practice existed from the beginning for this group as a discussion period following the lecture, a practice so entrenched that it was followed whether or not it was listed on the printed order of service. Guest speakers were told when invited that they would be expected to answer questions after their talk. The previous minister did not like the practice, feeling that it detracted from the impact of the service, and attempted to discontinue it. There were and are vigorous and vocal objections. A self-described "agnostic and humanist" refuses to attend when the talkback is omitted. Another long-term member gave an eloquent account of the history of talkback in the denomination to those attending a leadership retreat. When the newly called minister was under consideration, one of the first questions asked of her was her opinion on the issue. Talkback contains both elements that I have been describing for the set of mediating devices used by the Fellowship. It embodies the essentially social nature of their practice and, when prominently included in that practice, is symbolic of their differentiation from religion in general and Christian churches in particular.

As I mentioned briefly at the beginning, I now think that while there are many interesting questions about why and how Unitarian Universalism is growing in the South, the relative rate of that growth is an artifact of demographic change. Denominational research projects that for every one thousand people in the general population who have at least four years of college, there are four potential Unitarian Universalists, and local census figures support growth at approximately that ratio: the percentage of college graduates in the area has increased much more rapidly than population growth as a whole. Is "non-Christian as alien" also an artifact? Possibly. Perhaps it is a characteristic of this particular group, embodied in narratives of the non-Christian, nonnative founders and perpetuated in the dialectic of shared stories, individual and corporate. Stories I have heard at district events, however, suggest it is at least districtwide. Perhaps it is an artifact of my own story, an assimilation of the elements in the stories of others that confirm and reinforce my own sense of being, in my own home state, a "stranger in a strange land."

Part 3

Community Support, Control, and Identity

Christian Schools: Walking the Christian Walk the American Way

Melinda Bollar Wagner

Picture the Christian school of your mind's eye. What do you see? Children standing in rows, wearing red, white, and blue uniforms. The girls' skirts cover the knees; the sleeves of their blouses reach below the elbows. The boys sport white shirts, blue dress slacks, and navy ties. All are wearing black leather shoes that gleam with a spit polish shine.

The teacher calls out that it is time to go to chapel, and the children turn in their line as if they are one organism. But for knees raised not quite high enough, you would say they marched into the sanctuary where chapel is held. They quietly take their places, little ones in front, big ones in back; girls on the left, boys on the right. The chapel service will be led by the male pastor and principal, who lurks the halls never far from the paddle in his office.

What we tend to picture fits, in social science terms, the "total institution" model. The classic total institution—the prison or the traditional convent—controls nearly every aspect of people's lives, stripping them of any accoutrements of identity save those offered by the institution itself. Well-researched studies of Christian schools have said that the conservative Christian church and school is a total institution (Peshkin 1986; see also Parsons 1987, Rose 1988, and Wagner 1990 for more discussion of Christian schools). Indeed, if we listen to the words of the conservative Christians who have created the schools, we do hear talk of separation from the world; a favored expression is "Be ye not unequally yoked together with unbelievers" (2 Corinthians 6:14). Separate, polarized, and devoid of compromise—that is the picture of conservative Christianity that most of us hold in our minds.

Is this an accurate picture? Why should we care about what goes on inside Christian schools? Their tremendous growth has turned the spotlight of attention on them. Over the last twenty-five years, they have been the fastest growing sector of American education. Today at least one million students, representing one-quarter of all children enrolled in private schools, attend about ten thousand Christian schools.

In order to explore the culture within Christian schools, I undertook a year-and-a-half of full-time participant observation, with the help of grants from the National Science Foundation (Grant No. BNS8520070) and Radford University. My sample of Christian schools included all seven Christian schools in "Southeastern Valley," as the study area is called, plus two schools in the nearest city and two farther away. The schools were sponsored by independent Baptist, Wesleyan, Holiness, Pentecostal, and new charismatic churches; they thus covered the gamut of the fundamentalist, evangelical, and charismatic branches of the conservative Christian family tree.

One was my "home school," where I attended all functions from the August preschool workdays to the postschool workdays in June. I attended all morning faculty prayers, faculty meetings, all PTF (Parent/ Teacher Fellowship) meetings, board meetings, and sat in on classes from three to five days a week. I went along on all field trips, attended the parties, went to faculty luncheons and dinners, and talked to parents. At the other schools I sat in on classes and chapels, went on field trips, and attended ball games, Christmas programs, and graduation exercises. In all, the eleven observed schools had a combined enrollment of nearly two thousand students with 135 teachers, and I talked to some thirty more school administrators.

Three more samples of material were collected. Trips were made in a two-hundred-mile radius in every direction to attend national conventions of Christian educators and courses for Christian school teachers. The sponsoring organizations included A Beka Books, Accelerated Christian Education, the Association of Christian Schools International, the American Association of Christian Schools, and the Institute for Creation Research. Included here were discussions with leaders of the national organizations, regional sales representatives, and national marketing managers of curricula for Christian schools.

Additional information about other schools was gleaned through a "snowball sample" by corresponding with personnel I met at regional and national conferences (N = 17 schools altogether).

Finally, in order to gauge the extent to which Christian educators could rely on "Christian" rather than secular materials, an inventory was made of associations that support Christian schools, book sellers, purveyors of curricula, and magazines for Christian educators. Nearly one hundred organizations of this nature were identified, and primary printed information was collected from each. For background, I read conservative Christian books, listened to Christian radio and television, and visited Heritage USA, home of the PTL empire founded by Jim and Tammy Bakker.

Let me give you another picture of a Christian school—an alternative picture to the one I assumed earlier. A teacher is standing in front of her class of twelve students, leading them in unison chants of "Aaa Aaa Apple" and "Ih Ih Indian." Up high on the classroom walls are hung pictures of everyday items used to teach the vowel and consonant sounds—apples, balls, cats, dogs, and Indians. The young blonde teacher is wearing a skirt printed with huge red and yellow flowers. Her red high-heeled shoes are open-toed, revealing dark red toenails that match her shiny fingernails.

Later she asks students to come to her desk and read to her from their reading book, one at a time. When it is his turn, John comes up to the teacher's desk and wiggles so that his back faces her, his head peeping over his shoulder. "I can't read it!" he says. The teacher reaches for him (since he seems to be trying to make a get-away), as she says, "That's what we're here for, to *learn* how to read it."

The teacher, Mrs. Sherwood, is sitting on a chair made for first graders; as John stands beside her, his head is even with hers. She enfolds him in her arms, holding the book in front of him. It looks like a loving embrace, but it also reduces the blonde-haired boy's wiggling and keeps his eyes focused on the book.

When some of the students at their seats talk too loudly, the teacher says, "If you don't be quiet, Mrs. Sherwood will put your name on the board, and you'll have to sit at recess."

Now let me fill in some of the context of this scene. The reading lesson takes place in a combined classroom of first and second graders. While not unheard of in public schools, the combined classroom is common in small Christian schools. The classroom walls are filled with figures of Snoopy—some with scripture, some without—and large-headed, big-eyed children created by Joan Walsh Anglund,

Harry and David, and Precious Moments. The behavior modification forms of discipline (such as sitting during recess) were used very frequently, but Mrs. Sherwood might also say, "What does God say about that?" Before reading time began, the class had had a Bible lesson.

Like my social science colleagues, I *thought* that I would find fundamentalist Christian ideology—and only fundamentalist ideology—clearly played out in every aspect of the Christian schools. But as this scene and many others I could describe show, what I found instead is a tapestry woven from strands of American mainstream popular culture, professional education culture, *and* elements of Christian culture. The Christian alternative school is not as alternative as it could be. (See Hunter 1983 and 1987 for an analysis of other accommodations made by conservative Christians.)

Within the Christian schools, compromises are evident. This brand of fundamentalism was born in the United States and is in some ways overwhelmed by American popular culture. Inside the schools, American individualism, competition, and materialism coexist or compete with the gentle fruits of the spirit that the conservative Christians say they have as their goal: love, joy, peace, long-suffering, gentleness, goodness, faith, meekness, temperance (Galatians 5:22–23).

An analysis of the students' prayer requests—when they ask God for things—and praise reports—when they thank him for blessings they've received—showed that the pupils were much more likely to be concerned with trips to Disney World for themselves, or with teenage relationships, than they were with, say, the healing of others' bodies or souls. For example, 42 percent of the praise reports concerned themselves, and 44 percent praised God for an experience such as a sleepover or going to the toy store. In other words, the fact that they ask God for things has as its source conservative Christian ideology. But the things they ask God *for* are the things they've learned to want from American popular culture.

A professional educator from a secular school would feel right at home with the vocabulary and structure of the Christian school. In this microcosm of the professional education cultural scene, Christian teachers, using textbooks, ply their trade in school buildings that approximate as closely as possible public school buildings. The schools are in session five days a week, nine months of the year. The students are organized into grades; the curriculum is divided into subjects, in which students receive evaluations of A-B-C-D-F on report cards. Parents are asked to participate in Parent/Teacher Fellowship and are held at bay during parent/teacher conferences. Teachers attend workshops on critical thinking and obtain continuing education credits.

An analysis of discipline showed that techniques based on behavior modification ("You'll lose the points you have accumulated if you do that") were used much more often than those based on religious principle ("Jesus doesn't want you to do that"). The most often used were simply directives to do or not to do something. For example, "No talking please"; "Sit down, sit down, you all sit down"; "John, we don't need any duck sounds, sir"; "Oooh, don't put the scissors in your mouth, honey." On any given day, in any particular classroom, responses such as these accounted for 17 to 37 percent of the instances of discipline. The behavior modification techniques accounted for another 0 to 26 percent. Invoking God or Jesus—for example, "You're doing this for Jesus; you're not doing it for Mrs. Jones"; "Would Jesus be pleased if you spit on him?"—accounted for 0 to 3 percent of the instances of discipline. Corporal punishment, including threats, was used 0 to 3 percent of the time.

Analysis of how time is used in the schools showed that as much as 23 percent or as little as 3 percent of the students' day can be spent on religious studies and religious rituals.

The question then becomes, why do we find compromises rather than the expected total institution? On the one hand, the conservative Christians teach their children that they are a separate people, a people apart from the world. The little ones are taught to sing "Be careful little ears what you hear; be careful little eyes what you see." The older pupils are taught that "the devil is after your mind." Yet for all these exercises in polarization and boundary maintenance, the conservative Christians are well aware that they are compromising.

When the conservative Christians set about to open a Christian school, they are "building" a new culture (Ortner 1984). It would be instructive to view the creation of a Christian school as a "revitalization" process. In Wallace's terms, a revitalization movement is "any conscious, organized effort by members of a society to construct a more satisfying culture" (1966:39).

The interpretation of Christian school building as a revitalization process is close to the way the Christians themselves view their task. In

Wallace's terms, the conservative Christians' model of an ideal society would be their *"goal culture"* (1966:160). The *"existing culture,"* on the other hand, is seen as "inadequate or evil in certain respects" (160, emphasis his); for the conservative Christians, the American way of life, and particularly secular humanism, is the denigrated existing culture. The Christian schools themselves are the *"transfer culture,"* the crucible of change that connects the denigrated and the ideal. Inside the Christian schools the revitalization process—"the process by which cultural materials which have hitherto appeared to the members of a society as dissonant are analyzed and combined into a new structure"— is ongoing (211).

It should not be a surprise that conservative Christian educators create a school culture that borrows from the surrounding mainstream culture. How successful would a more "alternative" alternative be? Sahlins makes this point about new cultural forms, using the example of the fashion designer, who we *think* "plucks his ideas out of thin air" (1976:217). "But the fashion expert does not make his collection out of whole cloth; . . . he uses bits and pieces with an embedded significance from a previous existence to create an object that works, which is to say that sells—which is also to say that objectively synthesizes a relation between cultural categories, for in that lies its salability."

The Christian school must also "sell" its product. It must forge compromises that "objectively synthesize a relation between [competing] cultural categories." Christian school administrators voiced this necessity when they told me, "you can't take it all away" from the students. Their schools, homes, and churches, they said, are "not heaven," and compromises are made while "living on this earth." In constructing these compromises, the progenitors of Christian schools manifest a mode of thought discussed by Levi-Strauss.

Levi-Strauss (1966) made a distinction between the methods of the engineer, who plans what materials and resources are needed for a project and sets about to acquire them, and the *bricoleur,* the handyman jack-of-all-trades who works with what is at hand. He applied the term to the building of cultural forms as well as to technological labors. The Christian educators work in the *bricoleur* mode, picking and choosing from what's available, and making alterations to popular cultural themes and artifacts, rather than using an entirely new pattern to fashion alternative cultural forms out of whole cloth.

Thinking like the *bricoleur*'s opposite, the cultural engineer, we can imagine a process of clarifying the values the conservative Christians desire for their goal culture and then examining alternative ways to instill these in their children. For example, if the ideal goal culture is one where material goods and competition have little value, then how do you train children in that mode? (Remembering that the children are, at the same time, surrounded by the value that these things *do* have in American society.) Perhaps this would require an Amish-like isolation that these Christians are not willing to pursue. They do, after all, want their children to succeed *inside* American society.

Instead, like Levi-Strauss's *bricoleur,* they create Christian alternatives based on popular culture templates. Rather than abstaining from competition, Christian school organizations hold contests for finding Bible verses speedily. Rather than eschewing collecting toys, conservative Christians create My Little Ponies and Care Bears and Their Friends with Bible verses appliqued on them. The alternatives might better be described as alterations.

Accommodations are necessary for both the long-term survival of the conservative Christian culture within American society and for the short-term survival of the schools themselves. If the Christian walk is to be popular in American society, it must be walked the American way. In the early part of this century, theologian Ernst Troeltsch wrote that "the fact remains that all intransigence breaks down in practice and can only end in disaster. The history of Christianity itself is most instructive in this connection. It is, in the long run, a tremendous, continuous compromise between the utopian demands of the Kingdom of God and the permanent conditions of the actual human life" (Pauck 1968:78; Troeltsch 1960:511).

How do the conservative Christians square their view that they are separate from the world with the accommodations that they have made? The anthropologist, seeking analytic answers, looks to ways the compromises are adaptive for survival in the environment or ways they fit together into a pattern that reflects the most important ideas of the culture. But the conservative Christian ideology yields a different explanation.

For the conservative Christians, "walking the Christian walk" means that they are "daily being led" by God; if they will listen, God will direct their footsteps into the pattern he has ordained. This is no less true for the schools that God is thought to have "raised up." Thus, for the conservative Christians, the choices and compromises made within the Christian schools are ultimately ordained by God.

Whether or not the cultural diversity provided by conservative Christianity is good or bad, adaptive or maladaptive for American society will, in the long run, be a question for philosophers and social critics, and not for the anthropologist, whose job it is to describe and interpret a culture, to make the important concepts in one culture understandable to readers in another.

For the critics and the proponents of the New Christian Right, there is much to ponder. But for those who fear the conservative Christian culture, it may be well to remember that it is embedded in the American culture that surrounds and penetrates it. At the same time, perhaps that very embeddedness will prevent it from offering the mitigating influences to American culture's materialism and individualism that have been sought by social critics since Tocqueville.

Ministering to the Working Class: Evangelical Protestantism in Rural Appalachia

Mary Anglin

This essay compares two work settings in southern Appalachia—one, a coal mining operation in southwest Virginia, and the other, a mica processing factory in western Carolina—to examine the relationship between evangelical Protestantism and the articulation of dissent. The two settings offer different vantage points for an analysis of dissent, for the coal miners engaged in a protracted strike organized under the auspices of the United Mine Workers of America (UMWA), while the mica workers, lacking formal recourse, registered their grievances through informal means.

In both instances, however, contractions of national and regional economies amplified the force of industries that relied on exploitative labor strategies to offset rising costs of production. And in both cases, the concerns of men and women as workers merged with their affiliations as members of mountain communities: they struggled not only for job security and safer workplaces but also for a decent life for their families and neighbors. In laying claim to fair and equitable working conditions, and the continued viability of working-class mountain communities, mica and coal workers alike looked to the traditions of fundamentalist Christianity for sustenance.

In a tradition that harked back to the coalfield wars of the early twentieth century, miners and miner-preachers in southwest Virginia called on the Scriptures for moral justification as they fought for a contract that kept intact the regulations and benefits won by previous generations of union miners (Corbin 1981). Equally important, Pittston strikers engaged the discourses of evangelical Protestantism in their struggle to maintain a constant and nonviolent vigil over the course of nearly a year, when a new contract was agreed on by the Pittston Coal Company and the United Mine Workers of America.

By contrast, the workers at Moth Hill Mica Company had no opportunity for formal contract negotiations, and their access to factory owners/managers was confined, for the most part, to informal conversations and social visits. Nonetheless, the mica workers contested management policies and voiced concerns over working conditions, especially with respect to the issue of safety hazards in the factory. As with the Pittston miners, the mica workers were as concerned about job security in the economic chaos of the late twentieth century as they sought to maintain some measure of control over labor processes, and like the miners, Moth Hill workers made reference to the Bible as the foundation for their efforts to secure fair and just working conditions.

Rather than cast this discussion of coal miners and mica workers in terms of the timeworn debate about whether the religious traditions of the South inspire resistance or quiescence (Pope 1942; Gutman 1976; Billings 1990), this essay proposes a different set of questions to draw attention to the nuances of evangelical Protestantism as they inform life and work in the mountains. Such questions include: How have mica workers and coal miners employed discourses of evangelical Christianity in strategies of resistance? What do these discourses tell us about the constellations of power that frame work settings and working-class communities in the late twentieth century? How do they inform the meanings and practices of evangelical Protestantism?

The intent behind these questions is to find a means of analysis that would lend credence to everyday struggles without having to write large the heroism of working-class communities. This approach recognizes that mica workers and coal miners, like other workers, engaged in practices at times oppositional and at times complicitous with the aims and directives of company owners. In the unsettled economic times of the 1980s and 1990s, for example, fighting for one's livelihood meant accepting contract concessions and/or working to assure the profitability, and therefore viability, of mining divisions and factory departments, while not ceding further ground to the incursions of management. Such seemingly contradictory strategies are testament to "the complex workings of social power" in factories and communities in the late twentieth century, which warrant further investigation (Abu-Lughod 1990:42).

At the same time, this approach seeks not to reduce religious traditions to their effect on factories and mines but to propose a broader reading of evangelical Protestantism as an important dimension of daily life in Appalachia. In asking what workers find "worth fighting about," we widen the lens to examine not only the location of work within Appalachian communities but also, equally important, the weight of cultural traditions and local histories in those communities (Sacks 1989:543).

To return to the story of the Pittston coal miners, what motivated the miners to wage a strike for nearly a year was the company's blatant disregard for the people of southwest Virginia and the UMWA organization they had fought so hard to establish. By 1989, when the strike commenced, Pittston had laid off four thousand union miners from a work force of six thousand miners and was pressuring the UMWA to make concessions in contract negotiations over the remaining union jobs (Yancey 1990; Couto 1993). The final straw was Pittston's decision to cut off health care benefits for retired and disabled miners and miners' widows. To quote William Byrne, a spokesperson for Pittston, "It's like a credit card that expires. Theirs expired" (Hollyday 1989:14).

Those were fighting words but not just that. In the words of one sign, "Pittston hate[d] old people" (Giardina 1989b:12). In attacking miners' rights, the company desecrated the memory of the grandparents and parents who had struggled in the past for the union (Yarrow 1990).

The strike itself was a departure from the past, in which union strikers retaliated against the violence of "gun thugs" hired by the coal companies. In the 1989 strike, the union wagered the courage and discipline of the miners in a protracted display of nonviolent civil disobedience against the tactics of the Pittston Coal Company and its guards, Vance Security Company, the Virginia State Troopers, and the courts of the state of Virginia.

The miners negotiated this unwieldy context in large part through reliance on the religious traditions of the mountains. It was not simply that strikers sang such hymns as "Amazing Grace" on the picket lines or that miners and their supporters—friends, family, local businesses, and even local law enforcement—stood their ground "because we trust in the Lord. We got a lot of prayers behind us" (Hollyday 1989:14). More than this, the miners found their ground in a way of life that was equal parts union history and an ethics rooted in the Bible.

As heinous an act as was Pittston's revocation of the health care benefits of retired miners and miners' widows, the company's plan to work miners on Sundays elicited an equally strong reaction from the miners. When this issue was brought up at the stockholders' meeting at Pittston headquarters in Greenwich, Connecticut, company officials dismissed the charge with laughter and the comment that miners only used religion as a crutch in the strike. Such rhetoric was not lost on the strikers, one of whom responded, "I use church to get through work during the week. That's my crutch in life, the whole meaning of it, because I hope to go to a better place when this is over." Not to be outdone, a Pittston executive retorted, "Come to Greenwich," to the laughter and applause of his colleagues (Giardina 1989b:14).

The juxtaposing of the claims of the church with the prerogatives of the coal company made possible not only the dignified presence of miners at a meeting where they were ridiculed and their concerns misrepresented but also their long and steadfast observance of nonviolence in place of the coalfield wars of the past. Miners and their supporters engaged in acts of civil disobedience: occupying a coal processing plant and the local offices of the coal company; blocking the roads to the mines; and facing, unarmed, the ranks of state troopers who were so flagrantly abusive of the strikers that the Virginia State attorney took measures to curtail the activities of the troopers after watching news coverage of arrests at Pittston (Giardina 1989a).

For many of the strikers, this was the first time they had ever defied the law or faced arrest, and entertaining the possibility of doing so was itself a moral crisis resolved only by finding foundation in the Scriptures for defiance of the law in observance of a higher calling. The Israelites of the Old Testament and the apostles of the New Testament joined forces with contemporary examples such as Martin Luther King Jr. in the reckoning of the miners. To shore up the faith and determination of the strikers, ministers and deacons held services and prayer meetings, holding forth in local churches, picket lines, and the rallying ground known as Camp Solidarity. One miner-preacher, concerned about spiritual unity, erected a prayer tent near the entrance to one of the mines. Each time the tent was dismantled by Pittston guards, the strikers resurrected it as a way of "making a spiritual stand" (Hollyday 1989:22).

The strikers prevailed, enduring arrests and fines and living on strike funds that were a fraction of the salaries to which they were accustomed. In response to the strikers' nonviolent stance and the public relations campaign organized by the union, religious leaders from national as well as local denominations signed a statement of solidarity with the miners—and clergy from Pittston's backyard took a full page ad in the Greenwich newspaper to announce their endorsement of the union's cause. No less a luminary than Jesse Jackson appeared at Camp Solidarity to an enthusiastic reception by the strikers, and leaders from Poland's Solidarity appealed to the Bush administration on behalf of the Pittston miners.

But the miners were not unlike Sisyphus in having to abide continuous setbacks alongside the victories they fought so hard to achieve. When all was said and done, union contract notwithstanding, many of the striking miners were still without jobs. Those who were employed had to make do with a Sunday work clause and other concessions gained by Pittston in the negotiations.

By comparison, workers in the mica factory had neither a union nor formal opportunity to negotiate the terms of their employment at Moth Hill Mica Company. And while the high-grade coal produced from Pittston mines was in steady demand on the world market, mica was a mineral whose market had been eroded by technological innovations and foreign competition. Mica workers, in other words, had little leverage to exert in an industry on the wane.

Unlike the miners employed by Pittston, the salaries of Moth Hill workers were tied to the state minimum wage—below the federal standard—and the only benefit the company offered was the right to buy into a health insurance plan at group rates. In the frequent intervals where production orders dwindled and factory operations temporarily ceased, Moth Hill workers had only the unemployment checks provided them by the state of North Carolina. Thus, the terms under which the mica workers labored were vastly different from the coal miners at Pittston.

Like the coal miners, however, Moth Hill workers operated in an industry known to generations of their families and the rules that governed shopfloor activities were the result of struggles and negotiation over decades. Through departmental networks and informal interchange, Moth Hill employees subverted the authority of factory supervisors and managers, so much so that a supervisor once exclaimed to me that the only one in his department who would listen to him was his daughter. Moth Hill workers contested work assignments they considered disagreeable and, on occasion, openly confronted factory owners about the health hazards to which they were subjected in the factory. At the same time, workers asserted timeworn rights to a leave policy that enabled them to meet the demands of families and farms without jeopardizing job security and prevailed on departmental supervisors to keep them employed in the midst of declining work orders.

While the terms of employment for Moth Hill employees were meager at best, and control of the factory more overtly paternalistic than at Pittston, mica workers were not resigned to their fate nor quiescent. Like the Pittston strikers, Moth Hill employees struggled for job security, for some measure of control over their labor, and for dignity. As I came to understand over the course of my fieldwork in the factory, it was a measure of kin loyalties, family histories of mica work, and the claims of local working-class churches that underwrote the concerns of factory workers.

I learned of the importance of local churches to the daily activities of mica workers the first day I spent at Moth Hill. The question regularly put to me by factory workers curious about my presence there was "What church do you belong to?" This was just as routinely followed by an invitation to visit their churches, an invitation that I accepted by attending services at three area churches and becoming a regular attendee at one of them.

The question and the invitation were, I quickly came to realize, an effort to place me in the web of community ties and political loyalties in which the factory was embedded. Doctrinal issues formed the basis of many workplace conversations where my own background as an Episcopalian was placed in relation to varieties of Pentecostal and Baptist interpretations of Christian theology/practice around which workers, for the most part, aligned themselves. Such discussion evoked issues of class as well as theology in a region that had been visited by missionaries of mainline denominations that established local outposts among the poor. In the settlement in which the factory was located, for example, there was a Presbyterian church founded by medical missionaries in concert with local land barons, as well as the Methodist church established by the founders of Moth Hill. Moth Hill employees, for the most part, eschewed these as the churches of the wealthy and their pretenders. While my religious upbringing positioned me in the ranks of "the other," marked by questions about the exotica of Episcopalian ritual, my participation in local Baptist churches rendered me approachable, though still a stranger.

Long Hill Baptist Church, which I attended each week with one of the Moth Hill employees, was a church where working-class men and women came together to discuss their lives and experience fellowship. A Missionary Baptist Church, Long Hill's theology rested on the King James version of the Bible as the literal transmission of God's Word to the faithful. Rather than ministers formally trained in theological seminaries, the pastors of Long Hill had been called by God to preach the Word. The message they offered was about a world divided into the leagues of the damned and the saved, and the importance of the church as the path to salvation.

There were contradictory elements in the theology espoused at Long Hill Baptist Church. On the one hand, Long Hill upheld traditions of patriarchal authority within the church and outside it, exemplified by the preacher's constant reference to himself as "God's man in the pulpit" and overt symbolism of male leadership in all phases of the Sunday worship service and other church activities. In worship service and the discussions that attended it, the Bible was called on to support definitions of gender, sexuality, and family in which male dominance and gender/age hierarchies were presumed.

On the other hand, the history of Long Hill, as with other Missionary and Free Will Baptist churches in the mountains, was one of independent organizations that eschewed church councils and upheld the primacy of individual belief. Religious services were, in this construction, a place for exuberant displays of faith and personal testimonials, not the recounting of church dogma.

If evangelical Protestantism celebrated patriarchal authority as symbolized by a male god and vested in preachers and deacons as contemporary representatives, that authority was held in check lest the church no longer be responsive to its constituency. Churches voted preachers in and out according to their responsiveness to the needs of the community. Indeed, the preacher at Long Hill lost his position as "God's man" during the course of my field research.

In other words, contained within the theology and practices of Long Hill Baptist Church were elements of individualism, emotionalism, radical morality, and patriarchy: the foundations of "back talk" or "witnessing," which deconstructs relations of authority through personal testimony (Stewart 1990). The teacher and exegete for my Sunday school class of older women thus offered criticism of such preachers as Jim Bakker, whom she referred to as being "up to his eyeballs in sin" and having succumbed to his own sense of importance, as a way to counteract the inflated discourse of Long Hill's pastor. What remained supreme was *God's* authority. Those who disobeyed God, be they preacher or not, would burn in the eternal fires of hell. And "the church would still go on" (Anglin 1990:214).

In his study of the coalfield wars of the 1920s, David Corbin (1981) argued that it was the notion of God's perfection that enabled miners in West Virginia to oppose coal operators and company preachers in a bitter and protracted battle. The coal miners and mica workers of the nineties, I would argue, likewise presented their grievances in the language of evangelical traditions as a contest between "the children of God" and "the sinners."

It was the duty of the saved to testify to their faith—in the mica factory, on picket lines, and in their communities. At Moth Hill such testimonies came in the form of denunciations of the factory owner as a sinner bound for hell and in conversation about how their rights were violated in the factory. Up in the coalfields of Virginia strikers contested the heartlessness of Pittston officials through prayer tents, vigils, and other displays of faith.

Courage and deep-seated conviction notwithstanding, miners and mica workers faced the crisis of a world in which sinners prospered and the saved suffered for their belief. At Pittston and Moth Hill workers acted on their faith in myriad ways, challenging policies they considered unfair and upholding the memory of previous generations of kinspeople who had labored for these companies. In claiming religion as their crutch in life, miners and mica workers asserted the value of working-class communities and traditions despite their reckless treatment by company officials. While such may or may not constitute the stuff of revolution, it was testimony to the ways that workers in the southern mountains meet the challenges of economic restructuring with fortitude and with grace.

NOTE

This research was funded, in part, through an Appalachian Studies Fellowship from Berea College, a James Still Fellowship in Appalachian Studies from the University of Kentucky, and a National Women's Studies Association-Pergamon Press Scholarship in Women's Studies. A portion of this essay previously appeared in "Same Old Soup, Just Warmed Over: Pittston and the Remaking of Poverty in Appalachia," presented to the American Anthropological Association, San Francisco, California, December 2–6, 1992. The names of Pittston strikers mentioned herein refer only to those who have gone on record in previously published accounts of the strike, and all proper names used in reference to the mica industry are pseudonyms.

A Spiritual Storefront Church in Nashville: A Thaumaturgical Response to Racism and Social Stratification in the New South

Hans A. Baer

Despite the status of Nashville, Tennessee, as one of the prosperous financial, entertainment, educational, and religious centers of the New South, the persistence of institutional racism and poverty is evidenced by a multitude of storefront and house churches that one finds scattered throughout the various predominantly African American neighborhoods of the city. One of these is a nonpretentious storefront church called the Temple of Spiritual Truth (pseudonym), which is the focus of this essay. Since 1973, the Temple of Spiritual Truth has been housed in a flat-roofed concrete building situated several blocks from the gleaming skyscrapers of the downtown area and Tennessee State Capitol. A sign outside gives the name of the congregation and some related information but does not state the hours of religious services. Although I revisited the temple in November 1987, the period of 1978–79 will serve as the ethnographic present for purposes of this account of the congregation. Unless otherwise indicated, I refer to members of the temple and other Spiritual churches by pseudonyms.

This essay provides an overview of the history, socioreligious organization, and various religious services and other social events at the Temple of Spiritual Truth. The temple shares much in common with other storefront congregations in the African American community in that it substitutes high religious status for low socioeconomic status and provides its members with a familial-like support system and the means to ventilate their anxieties and frustrations. As part of the larger Spiritual movement, it attempts to provide both its members and clients of its healing system with magicoreligious rituals by which to overcome the problems associated with living in a racist and stratified society.

BLACK SPIRITUAL CHURCHES AS A RELIGIOUS MOVEMENT

The origins of African American Spiritual churches remain obscure. They appear to have emerged in various large cities of both the North and the South—particularly Chicago, New Orleans, Detroit, Kansas City, and New York—during the first quarter of this century. The Spiritual movement cannot be viewed simply as a black counterpart of white Spiritualism (Baer 1984; Jacobs and Kaslow 1991). While initially congregations affiliated with the movement referred to themselves as "Spiritualist," by the 1930s and 1940s most of them contracted this term to "Spiritual." As part of this process, African Americans adapted Spiritualism to their own experience. Consequently, much of the social structure, beliefs, and ritual content of Spiritual churches closely resemble those of other religious groups in the African American community, particularly the Baptists and Pentecostals (Baer and Singer 1992). Furthermore, Spiritual people in southern Louisiana, many of whom probably were reared as Catholics, added many elements from Catholicism and, at a somewhat subtle level, Voodoo or hoodoo. Somehow Spiritual churches in other parts of the country incorporated these elements.

The Spiritual movement has no central organization that defines dogma, ritual, and social structure. While many Spiritual congregations belong to a regional or national association, some choose to function independently from such formal ties. While associations sometimes try to impose certain rules, policies, and even dogmas on their constituent congregations, for the most part they fail to exert effective control. Instead, like many other religious movements, the Spiritual movement exhibits an "ideology of personal access to power" (Gerlach and Hine 1970:42–43). Theoretically, anyone who is touched by the Spirit can claim personal access to knowledge, truth, and authority.

Even more than their Sanctified (Holiness-Pentecostal) counterparts, Spiritual congregations tend to be housed in storefronts, apartments, house churches, and simple frame church structures. Spiritual churches have found their greatest appeal among lower- and working-class blacks. The larger Spiritual congregations, which are housed in impressive edifices, crosscut socioeconomic lines and attract upwardly mobile African Americans.

THE HISTORY AND SOCIORELIGIOUS ORGANIZATIONS
OF THE TEMPLE OF SPIRITUAL TRUTH

Spiritual churches in Nashville date back to the 1920s (Lockley 1936). The Temple of Spiritual Truth was established in 1965 by Bishop Frank Jones and his wife, Glenda. Both were reared as Baptists but became members of Sacred Heart Spiritual Temple—one of the oldest Spiritual congregations in Nashville. Glenda Jones decided to join Sacred Heart Spiritual Temple because she had been instructed by God to preach the gospel—something that she could not do in a Baptist church. Sacred Heart Spiritual Temple had been established by Bishop Ladner, a woman who also served as the overseer of a small association that included now-defunct congregations in Nashville and a congregation in Jackson, Tennessee. Frank Jones followed his wife into Sacred Heart, where he rose to the position of assistant pastor and she became an elder. Following the Spirit's instructions, in 1965 Frank and Glenda Jones held their first services in a funeral home chapel and for a while in their home. They affiliated their congregation with the Greater Universal Spiritual Unity Union (actual name) headquartered in St. Louis, an association that granted them "papers" to serve as bishops. They relocated their congregation to a storefront in 1967 and again in 1973 to its present location.

Although only a few dozen individuals may be present at the various services at the Temple of Spiritual Truth, it has a rather elaborate socioreligious organization. Bishop F. Jones serves as the pastor and Bishop G. Jones serves as the assistant pastor. Several men and women serve as elders, in which capacity they assist in conducting the service, including delivering occasional sermons. The congregation has several deacons and deaconesses who also assist in the conducting of services. The Temple has several missionaries—women who theoretically teach the gospel. During the service, they may be called on to say a prayer, give a sermonette, or monitor the testimony session. The choir, which is presided over by Bishop Glenda Jones, consists of several girls and two adolescent males. Various women and girls take turns serving as ushers. Bishop Glenda Jones also serves as the church treasurer and another woman serves as the church secretary.

RITUAL AND SOCIAL EVENTS AT THE TEMPLE OF SPIRITUAL TRUTH

Despite its humble exterior, the Temple of Spiritual Truth is a hub of activity for several dozen Nashvillians, some of whom visit it regularly and others who do so sporadically. Directly below the pulpit, which is situated on a stage elevated about a foot above the main floor, is a small folding table, covered with a white cloth, which serves as an altar. This table holds several statues of Catholic saints (including a large one of Saint Francis of Assisi), a large "seven-day" candle with a short prayer to St. Joseph inscribed on it, several small votive candles, a picture of Jesus, a large crucifix, a bowl of fruit, a plant, a small Bible, and several other items. A large statue of the Sacred Heart of Jesus stands near the entrance and on the walls hang various pictures, including one of the Blessed Virgin. Beyond the sanctuary, toward the rear of the building, are the offices of the pastor and the assistant pastor, a compact dining/ meeting room, and a small lavatory. During the course of religious services members frequently go to an office or meeting room to consult with the pastor concerning church affairs or to seek spiritual advice.

Although the sanctuary can seat 150 or so people, generally there are some 20 to 40 individuals present for the Sunday morning service. Special revival meetings may result in a larger attendance because members of other churches attend. While Bishop Glenda Jones begins the service, her husband often chauffeurs certain members of their flock in a well-used car, returning in time for the second half of the service, during which he generally delivers the sermon or "message." With a home-prepared meal, an afternoon program, and an evening service, Sundays are extremely busy days at the Temple of Spiritual Truth. The church also frequently holds Friday night services and occasional "bless services" at which Bishop F. Jones, his wife, or one of the mediums belonging to the congregation directs "messages" from the Spirit to various people present. Like most contemporary Spiritual churches, the Temple of Spiritual Truth does not conduct seances as did the early African American Spiritualist churches. Bishop F. Jones said that he tried to conduct a seance once but it failed because "hanky-panky" occurred during it. The Temple also conducts Bible study classes and special classes at which instruction in the performance of various rituals that the Joneses refer to as "mysteries" are taught. Although many of these classes are restricted to members of the congregation, Bishop F. Jones once invited me to attend such a class.

At this class, which occurred in the rear meeting room, F. Jones placed a small candle and a small dish at each participant's place. He passed around a vial labeled "Dr. Japo" and instructed each of us to anoint himself or herself. Next F. Jones instructed us to "dress" or "anoint" our candles with ointment from a vial marked "Love Luck" while twisting the candle upward, downward, and upward again in our hands. He then asked us to present the candle to Jesus, light it, and attach it to our dishes with the melting wax. We were instructed to close our eyes and to silently state our innermost desires. According to F. Jones, he can prophesy by examining the candle drippings that fall onto the dishes. At the end of the class each participant was asked to donate a dollar, although only two of us could afford to do so. During the second half of the meeting Bishop Glenda Jones delivered messages to several of the participants. As I left the class, F. Jones asked me, "Did you have fun?"

The congregation also conducts a wide variety of special events during the course of the year. Members collect funds in order to present Bishop F. Jones with money and gifts for the Pastor's Anniversary that is conducted in October or November. Ministers from other churches, both Spiritual and non-Spiritual, deliver sermonettes and commentaries extolling the pastor's achievements and virtues during this event. Bishops Frank and Glenda Jones observe the proceedings while sitting in easy chairs facing the congregation. The protracted evening service is followed by a banquet that continues into the early hours of the morning. The annual Homecoming hosts former members who have moved to other parts of the country and includes an elaborate potluck dinner and picture-taking of the congregation and guests. "Teas" involving singing and musical performances serve as fundraising events for the church. Occasionally the temple sponsors picnics and excursions to visit Spiritual churches in other cities.

PROPHECY AND "READINGS" IN THE TEMPLE OF SPIRITUAL TRUTH

Although Spiritual churches conduct many of the same religious services and rituals—such as testifying, shouting, and anointing the holy oil—that black Protestant groups do, their emphasis on prophecy is one of their distinguishing characteristics. Bishops Frank and Glenda Jones and a few other members of the Temple of Spiritual Truth serve as prophets, advisors, or mediums. In this capacity they function as intermediaries between the Holy Spirit and members of the congregation and clients who may belong to other churches. Prophecy or "readings" occur in one of two contexts: (1) a special religious service called a "bless service" or "prophecy service" and (2) a private consultation.

Bless Services at the Temple of Spiritual Truth

Many Spiritual churches schedule bless or prophecy services on a regular basis, such as every Wednesday evening. Bishops Frank and Glenda Jones schedule bless services as the Spirit directs them or one of the mediums belonging to the church to do so. Occasionally a traveling prophet or prophetess may conduct a bless service or give messages during the course of a revival meeting. Bishop Alma Scott, a heavy-set elderly woman, is one of the mediums who periodically conducts bless services at the Temple of Spiritual Truth. Over the years she belonged to various Spiritual churches in Nashville. Although Bishop Scott has been a member of the Temple of Spiritual Truth in the past, she belonged to another Spiritual church in Nashville when I first met her but rejoined the former later on during the course of my fieldwork. Bishop "John the Baptist" Evans is another medium at the Temple of Spiritual Truth. While in prison, a voice said to him, "John, you tell the world that I freed your soul." During the bless service the medium relates various aspects of the present, past, and future of selected individuals in the congregation. The medium may deliver the messages from the pulpit or the front portion of the sanctuary or he or she may move up and down the center aisle, selecting recipients for messages.

Bishops Frank and Glenda Jones as Spiritual Advisors

Like other Spiritual leaders, Bishop F. Jones is quite eclectic in his beliefs. He believes in reincarnation and studies books dealing with astrology, African religions, and Hinduism. F. Jones maintains that while the Catholic Church goes back to the time of the ancient Egyptians, the Spiritual church was started by Christ. He believes that Jesus can send the saints or the angels in the form of spirits to help people overcome their problems. Bishop F. Jones claims that Christ performed many "mysteries"—healings, prophecies, interpretations, etc. He said that the Lord gives certain people "secrets" so they can obtain spiritual power from themselves and others. The Lord provides the leader of a Spiritual church with "special secrets."

F. Jones claims that God gave him the gift of healing at nine years of age when an elderly woman was healed when he washed her feet. He sometimes uses blessed handkerchiefs and aprons in healing rituals because "some people have to have something that touches them to get a feeling of help." F. Jones applies oil or water in his healings, but stated that "while water can do the job itself," oil, especially olive oil, can "capture a person's mind because some people have to have something." If people have a "poison" in their bodies, he recommends that they drink an herbal tea.

Bishop F. Jones defines "counseling" as "something that you tell an individual that the Lord told you." Although he has a full-time job as a plumber and general handyman for a small construction company, F. Jones stated that he generally advises four or five clients a week. He advises clients primarily at his home but also in his church office and on the telephone. Many of his church members regularly call him on the telephone so that he will interpret their dreams. Bishop F. Jones claims that he can do more for a client than a psychologist because he derives his power from God.

Bishop Frank Jones listed three major categories of problems for which his clients seek advice: (1) domestic problems, (2) financial problems, and (3) alleged "voodoo" curses. F. Jones believes that, in the case of domestic problems, it is best to have both mates present for the consultation. The Spirit provides a "program" of budgetary management for those with financial problems. F. Jones maintains that some clients who claimed to be "voodoo" victims are suffering from some sort of psychological disturbance while others "got mixed up with the wrong kind of people and picked up a wrong spirit."

Bishop F. Jones said that he generally spends between fifteen and thirty minutes counseling each client. He joins hands with the client and prays to God for a message. F. Jones sometimes turns out the lights and burns a candle during a consultation. He also may give a client a candle for use at home. While in theory a candle is not necessary for communicating with the spirit world, it may help to focus the client's thoughts on overcoming his or her problems. F. Jones said that he "charges" fifteen dollars for private consultations. In addition, the client is expected to pay for any herbs, ointments, or other materials that may have been needed during the consultation. If a client requests that F. Jones visit him or her outside of Nashville to conduct a consultation, he or she must pay for the travel expenses incurred. If a client cannot afford to pay for a consultation, he or she is not turned down. Conversely, some clients pay more than the standard fee as a token of appreciation.

Bishop Glenda Jones also regularly conducts private consultations. When the Lord began speaking to her, she thought that she was losing her mind but now realizes that it is a "natural thing." As a young woman, G. Jones claims that she had lived a "natural life—drinking, traveling around, etc." A female drinking partner placed "snake dust" into her liquor, inducing extreme fear in G. Jones. The Lord "fixed" her through the ministrations of a "hoodoo man" in Alabama. As a result, G. Jones discarded "worldly things" and started to sing in the choir of a Baptist church. When a voice told her that she was in the wrong church, she began to attend services at the Sacred Heart Spiritual Temple. She studied for a certificate in "healing, preaching, and prophesying" under the tutelage of a Spiritual bishop in Indianapolis and has received additional training at Spiritual conventions.

Bishop G. Jones said that she does not allow her clients to tell her what is disturbing them. Instead, she prays and waits for the Spirit to "talk to me." As she supplies the client with various messages from the Spirit, the client is expected to reply, "Thank you, kind Spirit." On the small altar in her bedroom sit a white vase, a container of incense, a small red candle, and a soiled, open-faced Bible with six small crosses and crucifixes and an oval-shaped jewel. When G. Jones looks at one of the crosses or crucifixes, she receives "vibrations" concerning the present, past, or future of her clients. Toward the end of a consultation clients may ask questions of the Spirit. G. Jones estimated that about five clients come to see her personally and that from ten to fifteen clients contact her by telephone over the course of a week. She even counsels clients from as far away as New York and New Jersey. G. Jones stated that she spends about thirty minutes with each client, depending on his or her "conditions." Her "consultation fee" is ten dollars, but she accepts whatever the needy can afford to pay.

THE TEMPLE OF SPIRITUAL TRUTH AS A THAUMATURGICAL SECT

Like many other lower-class religious congregations, the Temple of Spiritual Truth substitutes religious for social status. Although one may occupy a humble standing in the larger society, a member of the Temple of Spiritual Truth may rise relatively easily to the position of evangelist, elder, deacon, deaconess, missionary, usher, choir member, or even prophet or prophetess. Women who are denied access to the pulpit in Baptist churches or other churches may obtain it at the Temple of Spiritual Truth. With its round of religious services and social events, the temple provides its members with a sense of *Gemeinschaft* or *communitas*. Individuals and families who might otherwise be isolated in the impersonal environment of the city become part of a fictive-kin network of "brothers" and "sisters." Group cohesiveness, although not always actualized, takes precedence over religious dogmas at the Temple of Spiritual Truth. The temple also provides its members and visitors with a variety of opportunities to ventilate their anxieties and frustrations, many of which derive ultimately from being poor African Americans in a racist and stratified society and having not been beneficiaries of economic development in the New South. Testimony sessions, which occur during most services and spontaneously from time to time, are occasions when members express their dependence on Bishops Frank and Glenda Jones and the congregation; they are expected to unburden themselves of recent disappointments and crises. Shouting—involving trancelike behavior, dancing, falling backward, running back and forth, leaping over pews, or even rolling on the floor—is actively encouraged by the ministers and apparently also serves a cathartic function.

Despite the functional similarities between Spiritual churches and other religious groups in the African American community, particularly those of the Baptist and Sanctified varieties, the emphasis on the manipulation of one's present condition through the use of magicoreligious practices distinguishes the former from the latter. The belief that events can be controlled through thaumaturgical practices is found in all walks of life, but especially among the poor, who often find themselves in a powerless situation. The acquisition of the "good life" and a slice of the American Dream are central concerns of members and clients of the Temple of Spiritual Truth as they are for other poor African Americans, many of whom have become members of a permanent underclass in a capitalist economy that treats them at best as part of a reserve labor pool. The intended function of thaumaturgical rituals is to put people in touch with supernatural power. As Robert Murphy asserts, magic usually promotes a sense of self-assurance and "produces the illusion that people are master of their fate, controller of their environment and not its pawn" (1979:170). In addition to magicoreligious rituals, such as burning candles, praying before images of Jesus, Mary, and the Catholic saints, and purification baths with Epsom salts, the Temple of Spiritual Truth provides its members and clients with a complex of prophets and advisors who dispense a sense of spiritual power and practical advice on how to cope with financial, domestic, and emotional problems—many of which are related to the conditions of poverty.

Unfortunately, the thaumaturgical approach to problem-solving promoted at the Temple of Spiritual Truth and other Spiritual churches tends to deny "political conflict by stressing the importance of the individual over society, the insignificance of social arrangement and plans, the irrelevance of group conflict beside the paramount importance of the individual" (Wilson 1978:356). Furthermore, like most Spiritual churches, the Temple of Spiritual Truth eschews social activism and inadvertently blames its members for their problems. In this regard it functions as a hegemonic institution that transmits the "cult of private life" championed by such agencies of socialization as families, schools, media, advertisers, social workers, and psychotherapists, deflecting attention from the social structural roots of racism and poverty (Greisman and Mayers 1977).

On 1 November 1987, I revisited the Temple of Spiritual Truth with Gordon Shepherd, a professor of sociology at the University of Central Arkansas, on our way home from the Society for the Scientific Study of Religion meetings in Louisville. Although Bishop Frank Jones seemed very much like I had last seen him over eight years earlier, he informed me that his wife, Glenda, had died three years ago. Her death appeared to have been a significant factor in the decline of membership at the temple. Bishop Jones, two middle-aged men, and a young woman occupied the elevated sacred area facing the congregation, and three women, a small boy, and the two visiting social scientists sat in the pews. Bishop Jones noted that he was not retired, but that the Lord always provides for his needs. He seemed delighted when I gave him a copy of my book on Spiritual churches (Baer 1984) and told him that he was included in it. As he thumbed through the book, while sitting in his episcopal chair, he asked me if he was really included in it. He gleefully smiled, and I was moved by his enthusiasm. To this day that incident serves as a reminder to me that ethnography can serve as a bond between people who come from very different worlds but share a common humanity. Transformation from observing the other to praxis and liberation, however, is the more critical issue.

"The Wind Blows, So Why Not Change?" Tradition, Change, and Transformation at Butler Street Baptist Church

Mona Taylor Phillips, Andrew Billingsley, and Fleda Mask Jackson

A blue river flows through blue-purple hills. This stained-glass image is above the baptistery, which is behind the choir loft and the pulpit. The baptistery, pulpit, and communion table (which is below the pulpit), are all draped in black material, outlined with strips of kente cloth. In the middle of all of the kente bindings there is the Ankh, the ancient Egyptian symbol of life. Six young African American men are walking around the pulpit, probably unaware that they are being photographed. They are greeting one another with handshakes and warm and easy smiles.

The challenge of accommodating, redefining, critiquing, *and* embracing the traditional—while introducing new ideas and new directions for the church—is the process dominating the character of Butler Street Baptist church in Atlanta, Georgia. Even the physical location of this small church of 587 members (381 active), centered in an emerging community of middle-income African American professionals, is a reflection of the same juxtaposition of old and new. The photograph described at the beginning of this essay is yet another representation of the dynamic process of pulling together and negotiating traditions—even redefining what is the traditional—and ensuring that the church becomes a useful haven for younger African Americans who are confronted with issues that are peculiar to this historical period.

RALPH MCGILL BOULEVARD: THE TRANSFORMATION
OF A CITY AND CHURCH COMMUNITY

Before talking about the minister and the programs in the church, it
is important that there be some understanding of the transformations
in the community surrounding the church—transformations that have
shaped and echoed some of the changes within the church itself. Butler
Street Baptist Church is officially documented as having "begun" on
the corner of Marietta Street and Thurmond Street in Atlanta, Georgia, in 1903, and having moved to Butler Street in 1904. However,
in an interview with Mrs. Lelia Mae Mattox, an eighty-three-year-old
member of the congregation who is affectionately referred to by church
members as the "professor," places the beginning of the church in
Livingston, Georgia (near Athens, where the University of Georgia is
located). Mrs. Mattox recounted, "I was born in Livingston, Georgia—
right below Athens. I came to Atlanta in 1936, but I joined Butler Street
in 1939. See, the former pastor of Butler Street was in the country, and
we used to go to his church there. So when I moved to Atlanta, I started
going to Butler Street since that's where he was."

Mrs. Mattox went on to describe Butler Street as an "old dirt road,
it wasn't paved." She does say that the street was paved when she got
to Atlanta, but some of the "old heads" told her about Peachtree Street
being "just gullies, nothing paved." Mrs. Mattox talks about the life
of Butler Street Baptist Church even before she herself was part of the
Butler Street that exists now. The fact that her personal memory of Butler Street Baptist Church extends beyond her personal involvement with
the church is striking, and it is an extended memory that is shared by
some of the other older members of the church. The church has had
only three ministers, two of whom served over thirty years. The wife
of one of the former ministers still attends the church. Therefore there
is a community of older people within the larger church who share this
extended memory, who have experienced only two ministers before the
current minister, and who contextualize their experience of the history
of the church within the larger history of Atlanta.

Butler Street Baptist Church is now on McGill Boulevard, surrounded
by complexes of condos and apartment homes, newly built within the
last ten years. Across the street from the church are tennis and basketball
courts, which are full on warm Sundays. A block east from the church

is the city's civic arena, and several blocks up from the Civic Center is an area of Peachtree Street littered by half-decimated old buildings, surrounded by gleaming glass and chrome hotels, bank buildings, retail stores, and expensive restaurants. Adjacent to the new condominiums and apartment homes, which are clearly designed for middle-income professionals and are primarily occupied by African Americans who fit that description, are neighborhoods of older homes and apartment buildings, many in desperate need of renovation and repair. These buildings are occupied by a mixture of low-income African Americans and whites. Mrs. Mattox talks about the recent changes in the area surrounding Butler Street with a voice full of dismay: "Our church got burned up. You know, Ralph McGill used to be Forest Avenue. So, we moved out of the church, and were having service on Forest Avenue in Forest Avenue school."

Mrs. Mattox describes the present church location as one purchased from the city Housing Authority, and one that they have occupied for the last twenty years. She goes on to describe the urban renewal and improvement projects of the 1970s and 1980s, which included the Civic Center, newer housing, and expressways, as transforming the community surrounding the church and changing the lives of the members of the church: "And after we got it [the building] through the Housing Authority, old Russell [Herman Russell, a prominent African American developer] came through there and built all them condos. He wanted our church. Yeah, he wanted our church. Before the condos there were residential homes, a big school . . . so they tore the school down, and built a Marta station, then they put up that Civic Center. That's when they starting tearing down those homes."

Some of the homes of members of the church were bought out during the renewal process, but while they no longer live in the community, they are still members of the church. Mrs. Mattox spoke wistfully of the time when homes, as opposed to condos, surrounded the church, and also spoke with regret about the loss of a dental college that was also part of the community: "There used to be a dental college—Atlanta Dental College up there on the corner of Piedmont and McGill, which used to be Forest Avenue, you know. And you used to be able to get your teeth drawn and everything, like Grady [hospital]. But now that's gone. Marta came through and started tearing up."

Getting a sense of the history of the church's community does two important things. First, it gives a view of the loss experienced by the older members of the church. It is possible that the loss that may be felt when the minister gives a sermon challenging traditional notions about the race of Jesus and the sex/gender of God is as much a result of cumulative shifts and changes in older members' communities (and their extended memories about the church community) as well as the specific challenge to deeply held ideas about Jesus and God.

Just as knowing the history of the church as that history has been experienced by the older members of the church provides a basis for understanding how the church feels to older people, such knowledge also provides some grounding for beginning to understand how the younger people in the church experience the church very differently from the older individuals. Younger people have their own experiences rooted in their specific generational realities. But the fact that there is no "before" or "used to" for many of the younger people in the church (and we are defining younger as up to forty years old) also means that their responses to new ideas and to change is a reflection not only of their age but also of their relationship, which is determined by their age, to the history of the church.

REVEREND A. PARKER: AFRICAN-CENTERED TRADITIONALISM

"We want to proceed right to the heart of the Gospel. Because at the heart of the Gospel is Jesus . . . a real man, of a real place, with real ancestors, interacting with real people. Our question for today is who is this person? When an African American, who also claims to be a Christian, says that it doesn't matter what color Jesus is, he or she is speaking out of total ignorance of history and of the importance of symbols in our lives. He or she is saying, in effect, that any religious symbol will do" (Parker 1992).

Reverend Aaron Parker, the thirty-eight-year-old minister of Butler Street, speaks in slow, deliberate cadences with carefully chosen words about his ideas concerning the role of black churches in an increasingly complex society for black people—especially younger black people. He is one of the more popular and well-liked professors at Morehouse College, an all-male historically black college in Atlanta. The Reverend Parker, who has a degree in systematic theology from the Candler School of Theology at Emory University, is firm in his conviction that some changes are necessary for black churches to remain vibrant institutions within African American communities. His particular vision for Butler Street is that it one day becomes an economic resource for individuals who wish to start businesses—so they do not have to "go begging to banks." He sometimes admonishes the congregation during Sunday services that "new problems require new ways of doing things," and that "if you want to get rid of me, that's fine, but we must rethink the way we do things." While working within the traditional structure of the church (many of the old governing bodies and committees have remained intact: Mothers' Board, Board of Deacons, etc.), the Reverend Parker uses sermons, Bible study sessions, and visual representations to challenge traditional conceptualizations of God, Jesus, and the meaning and purpose of religion in the life of the African American community. For example, in the sermon "Why a White Jesus Won't Work," Parker traced the genealogy of Jesus (as that genealogy is written in the Bible) and placed the figure of Jesus within a specific sociohistorical context. He asked the congregation to think about the origins of a "Europeanized" representation of Jesus. When asked the importance of the color of Jesus, the Reverend Parker responded, once again, choosing his words very carefully, that "a people who does not worship someone who looks like them is inclined to think badly of themselves and their group." The lively response of the congregation to the sermon about the racial imagery of Jesus is perhaps indicative of support and agreement. However, as Parker specifically spoke to the fact that some of the members of the congregation had pictures of "blue-eyed, blond Jesuses in their homes, over their beds," [1] one of the older women of the church rocked slowly on the back pew, shaking her head, muttering, "Lord, Jesus. Help us in here today."

The very next Sunday the sermon focused on the gender representation of God. Parker entered that discussion by asserting that considering the "patriarchal society out of which the Bible came, it would make sense that God would be male." The Reverend Parker asks the congregation to consider biblical text within a sociohistorical context by asking that they consider their particular culture, and the specific location of women within that culture. The Reverend Parker, through the use of examples culled from the everyday and historical experiences of African American people, suggested that black women have a centrality in African American culture and called for a reconsideration of the traditional conceptualization of God as man. He prodded the congregation into thinking about the role of "mother god"—god as guide, protector, source of wisdom—much like the mothers in their own lives. When asked, the Reverend Parker noted that he thought that the response of the congregation was a "good" one to the sermon about God as woman. In fact, he suggested that there is a preexisting base in African American culture that would not make the notion of God as woman a particularly alien or disquieting idea. The church's orientation and membership manual, which outlines the goals, programs, history, and basic doctrines of the church, reads: "God—a. We believe that God (Elohim, Yehovah, YHWH, Theos) is the creator of this universe, including human beings. As creator, God is the ultimate source of our being and well-being. Furthermore, as creator, God relates to us in what we might symbolically call Father and Mother (See Genesis 1 and 2)."

Therefore, new symbols and reconstructed meanings are sprinkled among the traditional elements of Butler Street Baptist church—new symbols and reconstructed meanings designed to place the practice and theology of Christianity within an African American context. A regular feature of the printed program every Sunday, positioned above the list of the "known sick and shut-ins," is the symbol of the Ankh, which is explained in the program as the Egyptian precursor to the crucifix. The walls of the rooms where Bible study sessions are held are covered with pictures of black representations of Jesus.

Parker's youth, affiliation with Morehouse College (which is part of the Atlanta University Center complex, a consortium of five historically black colleges and universities), and his African-centered ministry attract younger, educated people to the church. It must be emphasized, however, that all that is new which is introduced by Parker and other members of the church is introduced within the framework of what is considered the traditional. For example, all sermons, even the ones asserting that to worship a white Jesus is to worship white people, are delivered in the usual revival style of black baptist preachers. Bible study sessions, during which biblical text is examined as an inspired historical document, begins with prayer led by an elder deacon or mother. The Mothers' Board holds its dinners and meetings on the same nights that NIA, a support group organized by younger women in the congregation, holds its meetings.

Butler Street Baptist Church, in its institutional and ideological negotiations of the crosscurrents of change and tradition, strives to remain rooted in a redefined and expanded set of traditions, expanded to include elements of the African ancestry of the church members. This delicate balancing was articulated in the Reverend Parker's closing remarks at the end of the yearly spring recital sponsored by the Nurses' Guild, an association within the church whose membership consists of primarily older women. After having been firmly chastised by some of the members for disbanding the Senior Choir, Parker (1992) commented, "Let us thank God that we have made it through another Nurses' Guild Spring Musical. You know, I was raised in Canton, Mississippi, by a father who was a Baptist minister, and a grandfather who was a Baptist minister. And one thing I learned by watching them: That there are some things you don't bother. There are some things you leave alone. The Nurses' Guild you don't bother."

NOTES

This paper is based on observation and interviews in the Butler Street Baptist Church, Atlanta, Georgia, during 1992 and 1993 and is part of a larger, national study of community outreach programs in the black church conducted by Andrew Billingsley. The authors would like to thank Daryl White for invaluable insight and comments. "The wind blows, so why not change?" is quoted from Mrs. Gertrude Barnett, daughter of Mrs. Mattox.

1. The Reverend Parker acknowledged in an interview that the church was still dealing with issues of male dominance and control. For example, all the associate ministers are, at this time, male. What is interesting, and probably not unusual, is the degree to which the women of the church control and manage the church's business, including its financial matters, but still do not have positions of leadership during the Sunday service.

Returning to the Source:
Yoruba Religion in the South

Beatriz Morales

This essay describes the complex relationship between culture, identity, and religion through the examination of the life history of Baba Kunle, a Panamanian of African descent who established the Yoruba Temple in Atlanta. I propose that religion is not only an individual quest for spirituality but also the reaffirmation and reinforcement of ethnic identity in times of rapid political and economic change. In Baba Kunle's life it is possible to trace the significant events that led to the development of his current identity. His search for spirituality and identity took him from the North on a journey to South Carolina and eventually to Atlanta, where he established his own Yoruba Temple. He represents the transformations that many young African American men in urban cities underwent in the 1970s in their search for cultural identity.

The Ibeji Temple, located in an African American community in Atlanta, has more than one hundred members. Temple members hold annual festivals, which others in the community also attend. The Ibeji Temple is multicultural, with its members coming from Latin America and the Caribbean as well as the United States. The religious community of the Ibeji Temple is a microcosm of Africans from all over the world.

I met Baba Kunle when I moved to Atlanta from New Orleans where several members of the Ibeji Temple lived. Eva, a Voodoo priestess in New Orleans, invited me to the temple to meet Baba Kunle the day of her initiation into the priesthood of Oya. After many conversations, Baba Kunle invited me to assist in the creation of a Yoruba cultural center that he hoped to establish in Atlanta. I agreed to help by assisting with the documentation of Baba Kunle's temple and personal history.

124

THE YORUBA MOVEMENT IN THE AMERICAS

In the middle of the 1700s the religion of the Yoruba was carried to plantations in the Caribbean and Latin America by Africans taken as slaves from the Yoruba and Congolese areas of Africa. In the eighteenth century the kingdom of Oyo in Yorubaland, which controlled extensive territories with a powerful cavalry, was a major supplier of slaves. The kingdom finally fell when internal conflicts arose between the king, the Alafin, and the hereditary nobility. The final decline of the old Oyo empire resulted in the selling of many powerful priests and priestesses into the slave trade. The cultural survival of the Yoruba priesthood ensured the continuity of a Yoruba identity in the Americas. It was the Yoruba priests and priestesses who communicated with the *Orishas,* Yoruba divinities, and conducted the proper rituals to ensure the survival of the slave community. Today Yoruba religion is found in Brazil, Trinidad, and Cuba. An important aspect of the Yoruba religious movement in the Americas has been its blending with other religious systems. Yoruba religion was able to flourish hidden behind the veil of the Catholic church even during slavery. The mixing of Catholic saints and Yoruba Orishas is one of the distinctive characteristics of the Cuban Yoruba religion known as *Lucumi* or Santeria. However, Yoruba religious rituals and ceremonies maintain a sense of Yoruba ethnic identity regardless of their interaction with Catholicism.

YORUBA RELIGION IN THE NORTH

Beginning in the 1960s, the Yoruba religious tradition was carried to the United States by Cuban immigrants. Prior to the arrival of Santeria, Lucumi, a more traditional Yoruba form, was practiced among small groups of Afro-Cuban families in New York (Morales 1990). New York City in the 1970s was the Mecca of North American Santeria (Bascom 1972). With the emergence of the black power movement during the 1960s, African Americans began to enter the Santeria religion. According to George Brandon (1991), earlier redefinition of African American cultural identity countered the stereotype of a lost African identity. As the movement for democratic rights grew, the demand increased for the legitimization of African American identity in terms of its African heritage. The Cuban Santeria religious tradition grew and was transformed in the context of the African American urban experience. Brandon (1991) points out that Orisha-Voodoo, which emerged from Santeria in New York in the 1960s, was the result of larger economic and political changes taking place in the African American community.

A significant transformation of Santeria took place in New York with the development of Orisha-Voodoo, which began under the leadership of Oba Ofuntola Oseijiman Adelabu Adefunmi I.[1] Born Walter King in Detroit, Michigan, he was introduced to Santeria and went to Cuba in 1959 to become the first African American initiated into the Orisha priesthood. He began a process of rearranging and rebuilding the Santeria religion to suit the needs of African Americans. This process of cultural transformations contributed to the emergence of Orisha-Voodoo, a new religious variation that placed more emphasis on African cultural identity than on the ritual practices of Santeria. Oba Oseijiman introduced revolutionary changes, such as the performance of ritual ceremonies in public, wearing African clothes, and taking African names before entering the Orisha priesthood. He and his followers openly opposed the religious syncretism between the Orishas and Catholic saints that characterized the Santeria religion. In contrast, Orisha-Voodoo represents the mixing of the Orisha and Voodoo pantheons and considers the devotion to Catholic saints unacceptable because it is viewed as an attempt to force the Yoruba religion into a Western framework (Brandon 1991; Hunt 1979).

Oba Oseijiman and his Orisha-Voodoo followers began feeling pressure to conform to the dominant Santeria religion. Cuban priests and priestesses resented the movement not only because it played down the role of the Catholic saints but also because it questioned the legitimacy of Christian influences. The Oba decided that he needed to move out of New York City to find a sacred place in which to establish Orisha-Voodoo. By 1969 he had moved his temple to the South because he considered the social order there to be more conducive for building African culture on United States soil (Cohen 1973). He founded the Oyotunji Village, an African community in rural South Carolina.

THE AFRICAN VILLAGE IN SOUTH CAROLINA

The village is now called Oyotunji, which means "the ancient city of Oyo returned" (Oyo is a major Yoruba city in Nigeria). The Oba chose that name because he had a vision that Afro-Cubans and African Americans were descendants of people from Oyo. Oyotunji is a re-creation of an African village with the social organization of the village modeled after the African monarchy. The Yoruba traditional religion guides all social relations. All village resources are controlled by the Oba, who has final authority over everyone. Democracy was rejected because it embodied too many internal contradictions. One of the major shrines in the village is that of *Dambada Hwedo,* which is dedicated to Africans who died during slavery and did not receive an African burial. Although the Oba began by modeling family life in the village after the traditional African family, he found it impossible to implement. Women in the village, protesting the traditional place of African women as too subservient, fought for more power. Today, the most important political positions in the village are held by women (Hunt 1979).

THE YORUBA TEMPLE IN ATLANTA

The Ibeji Temple priest, Baba Kunle, is a descendant of Oyotunji. He is introduced as the Baba or head of the Temple and the most senior religious position in the household. Baba Kunle, the head of the Ibeji Temple, was among the first individuals to be initiated into the Orisha priesthood in Oyotunji. As such, he is part of the original core that contributed to the establishment of the village. He speaks of the Oba as a prophet whose name, visions, and personal life history he has tried to emulate. The ritual leadership of the Oyotunji village requires new devotees, priests, and priestesses to accept the Oba as the supreme leader of the Yoruba tradition in the United States. The Ibeji Temple in Atlanta works in close cooperation with Oyotunji. Ritual ceremonies, including the initiation of priests and priestesses, promotions, and annual celebrations of the Orishas' birthdays, are supervised by the central leader and his officials. Baba Kunle tells us how he felt on first hearing of the Oba in South Carolina: "I heard of an Afro-American, initiated into Santeria in Cuba, that was starting an African movement in South Carolina. At [that] point in my life, I was not seeking a religion, yet I felt I needed to go to South Carolina and help this man build his town for us [African Americans] to have further identity" (Baba Kunle 1991).

After going to live in the village, Baba Kunle began his spiritual journey that for the first time provided him with a sense of who he is as a person of African descent: "My walk to this life in the Yoruba culture started when I moved to the village. The Oba would regularly read to us or give us lectures on various different things of African systems and the Yoruba systems and it was the first time I had heard any of that because these things were not taught in schools or any place else. Our parents were not even qualified to teach us this because they were not educated according to such awareness" (Baba Kunle 1991). When Baba Kunle discovered this more Afrocentric form of Santeria known as Orisha-Voodoo, he felt that he could get closer to true spiritual realities. Indeed, Orisha-Voodoo is closer to Baba Kunle's own world view.

Baba Kunle recalls that although his parents did not practice any religion, he, as a child, was very religious. He felt early in life that he had a very special "gift" that made him susceptible to certain religious emotions. The spiritual energy that he received from interacting with the divine world awakened his desire to be a priest: "It was something that was just within me. It was many years later, after my trip to South Carolina and having the divination that those feelings came to head because it was spoken in that divination that spirits were guiding me into these different avenues and the reason that I would feel drawn to these places was that my spirit will guide me there" (Baba Kunle 1991).

He began to feel a special calling from the Orishas that prevented him from leaving the village. Finally Baba Kunle felt the power of the Orishas by entering the Oshun priesthood:

> It was never my intention to be initiated into Oshun or any deity. I just wanted to be a free agent moving around in the culture and participating in the unification of black people. However, a year after I found myself pulled right back to that village when they were in the process of clearing land to have a place for people of African descent to visit or learn about themselves or to live there if they want to, free of charge. The village was just beginning. . . . The organization and the new things that I was learning about myself as a person of African descent was so stimulating that although I could not see myself living in the country, being an urban person, yet I could not leave. (Baba Kunle 1991)

According to Baba Kunle, Orishas and ancestral spirits guided him to South Carolina and later to Africa. For it was in the South, not the

North, that Baba Kunle prepared for his journey to the motherland. In Africa he found his mission in life. He notes how an African priest explained to him his mission in the religion:

> During that particular trip an elder named Edgealonibu, a *Babalo- wou* and also a priest of *Obabatala* became the first elder that I met in Nigeria. We called him by the title *Babaibeji* meaning the father of twins. Of course, in the Yoruba culture the twins are so sacred. Although he was a father of twins and a priest we called him by his most revered name, father of twins. He told me that the *Orisha* sent me to embark on a responsible life in this culture and tradition and it was important for me to pass my experience on to other people who are looking for culture and tradition. He said I should name my temple Ibeji Temple because my temple will be blessed with a lot of children. That was my mission. (Baba Kunle 1991)

It is Baba Kunle's goal to build a cultural center for children in which he could not only teach African culture, philosophy, and tradition but also provide positive role models for children of African descent. These were not available when he was growing up.

Baba Kunle has taken his mission very seriously and twice a year he organizes large African festivals for his local community in Atlanta. The African procession of the Oba and his court through urban streets demonstrates to the community the aesthetic beauty of the Yoruba religion. As the Oba and his court parade through the streets, people are attracted by the ornate African clothing worn by the Oba and the priest and priestess as well as the singers and drummers. These festivals provide this low-income community with the opportunity to enjoy and experience a celebration of African heritage.

According to my analysis, the Ibeji Temple is shifting from the Orisha-Voodoo tradition and moving toward Santeria as Atlanta becomes a more multicultural city. When the temple first opened, the members were typically African American. New members, however, are predominantly Latinos. As Baba Kunle reflected on the spiritual needs of new Latino immigrants, he realized that the Orisha-Voodoo emphasis on black identity did not express the sentiment of the new immigrant population. As a result, Baba Kunle established closer ties with the

Santeria community. New members of the temple can be initiated into either Santeria or Orisha-Voodoo traditions. Members of both of these traditions treat each other as equals in the temple.

For Baba Kunle, these are both distinctive styles to communicate with the Orishas. It appears that Baba Kunle's bicultural upbringing allows him to synthesize two opposing religious forms into a new cohesive tradition. Baba Kunle continues, however, to identify his religion as Orisha-Voodoo because it expresses his black nationalist sentiment and supports the desire for self-determination—an important value in African American culture. He has adapted these values to life in the United States.

His identity, though, is not only based on race but also on ethnicity. His adaptation of Santeria demonstrates his recognition that one can retain ethnic identity while becoming part of the larger society. Santeria has a dual heritage, historically acting as a medium between Catholicism and Yoruba religion, which has allowed Baba Kunle to express his bicultural identity as both a Latino and an African American.

Orisha-Voodoo provides African Americans with a strong sense of African identity. As a new religion it emerged to express the value of self-determination. Orisha-Voodoo, however, can only provide individuals with a single identity. The Baba Kunle case illustrates how a single identity was too limiting in an urban multicultural environment. Baba Kunle drew on his bicultural background, and Santeria provided him with the ideal vehicle to meet the needs of an ethnically diverse community.

NOTE

1. *Oba* traditionally referred to a Yoruba king and to all the concepts involved with divine kingship. In this essay use of the term is meant to re-create those concepts for a congregation with ties to Africa. The title is passed from father to son.

Part 4

*Integrating Religious and
Regional Identities*

American Hinduism in the South:
Social Identity and Public Discourse

Michael V. Angrosino

This essay explores the ways in which the Bible Belt is giving way to the Sun Belt through the introduction of non-Christian religious beliefs and practices in a large southern city—Tampa, Florida. Although religion is certainly a conservative element in ethnic identification, it can also play a dynamic role in the construction of the multicultural urban New South.

I focus on the development of a community of immigrants from India to the United States (Indo-Americans) who are evolving a distinctive form of American Hinduism as a way not only of preserving their cultural distinctiveness but also of exerting some influence on the city's public policy in such fields as education, health care, and business. My analysis is based on data collected in the course of conducting an oral history of the Hindu Temple of Florida (HTF), a group to be discussed below. That project was part of a comprehensive survey of religions in the Tampa Bay area conducted in 1991 under the auspices of the National Conference of Christians and Jews (NCCJ) (Katz 1991). I also draw on my two decades of ethnographic research among Indian migrants in various parts of the Americas (for example, Angrosino 1983).

Asians compose approximately 1.5 percent of the population of the Tampa standard metropolitan area. Estimates of Indians specifically range from ten thousand to twenty thousand, most of whom live in the city of Tampa itself. Tampa's Indians are part of the extensive "second wave" of Asian immigration to the United States that began with the reform of the immigration laws in 1965. "Second wave" immigrants, to borrow a phrase coined by Fenton (1988:9), are typically well-educated, often professionally trained men and women who migrate as family groups. "First wave" Asians, by contrast, were usually single, uneducated men who found employment as manual laborers (Takaki 1989:420, 445–46). Indo-Americans tend to be treated as part of the generalized Asian "model minority" (Yun 1989) because they are perceived as hard-working, prosperous, law-abiding, and conservative in their social and political habits. There is undoubtedly prejudice against Asians in Tampa, but it is neither as widespread nor as virulent as that directed against less favored minorities. Moreover, friction between Asians and less favored minorities has not yet reached the flash point, as it has in other large cities.

Indo-Americans are drawn from the urban, secularized elite of India, and only one-third from a Hindu background identify themselves as Hindus in the United States (Kosmin 1991:4). Nevertheless, three-fourths report being "religious" (Fenton 1988:50), a pattern found in Tampa as well (Katz 1991:9). This apparent paradox is not unlike that described by Bellah and his colleagues (1985:219) for Americans in general, who like to consider themselves to be spiritual even if not affiliated with a formal religious organization. The Indians consciously stand apart from the orthodoxy of Hinduism but feel themselves to be the privileged vessels of the spiritual and ethical values represented by the Hindu tradition—values they hope to impart both to their children and to the society in which they now live. They often compare themselves with American Jews, whom they see as proudly identifying with Jewish history and culture even though they are not necessarily observant practitioners of the orthodox faith. The Indians are quite happy to participate in American life. But they do not want their children to be swamped by what they see as the excessive materialism, individualism, and competitiveness of American culture, and they actively seek to temper those tendencies by means of their "Oriental" outlook on life.

Aspects of the emergent American Hinduism have been analyzed in various parts of North America by Fenton (1988), Jensen (1988), Taub (1976), and Williams (1988). My remarks here, however, refer to practices observed specifically in Tampa. First, we must consider three sociodemographic factors: (1) American Hinduism is a minority religion; (2) the large joint family of Indian tradition has been supplanted by a more typically American nuclear family household; and (3) the extensive network of priests and ritual specialists typical of India was not transported to the United States.

These three factors mean that Indian parents cannot rely on their children being able to absorb their culture from a wider milieu; indeed, the wider milieu to which the children are exposed is explicitly non-Hindu. As a result, young adults—even if they are secularized professionals— have become much more actively engaged in the religious life of the community than would have been the case in India. Their involvement, however, has come to resemble that of other middle-class Americans; it is a matter of using church affiliation to promote positive civic virtues (e.g., collecting clothes for the needy) rather than to engage in private meditation or spiritual development.

Indian Hinduism is remarkable for its diversity. But the middle-class, religious (though not observant) Indo-Americans described above have long since learned that, as a minority, they can more efficiently represent themselves if they speak with a single voice. As a result, the multifarious manifestations of Hinduism are being homogenized into a set of practices and beliefs that can be commonly articulated—usually in English, rather than in an Indian language—and that derive from those found all over India, rather than from those specific to a particular region or caste. American Hinduism, therefore, sees itself as an ecumenical (i.e., nonsectarian) force. Many of the informants in Tampa prefer to drop the term "Hindu" altogether because it has too many associations with conditions specific to India; they prefer the generic term "Sanatana Dharma" (eternal truth).

The most important sociocultural modification of American Hinduism results from the fact that Indo-Americans have essentially dropped the institution of caste except in matters of marital arrangement. In India, caste regulates not only marriage but also residence, occupation, and a complex of ritual pollution that dictates dietary practices, social interactions, and a thousand other niceties of day-to-day living. Without caste, then, American Hinduism is becoming like "Sunday Christianity"—a set of beliefs and observances that are given special attention at designated times and in set-aside places but that no longer pervade every aspect of a community's life.

Moreover, the ritual cycle of Hinduism has been modified to fit American conditions. Gone are the enormous public festivals with their hundreds of thousands of devotees and gigantic temple processions. Even the numerous *samskaras* (rites of passage) have been substantially scaled back. Major festivals are now celebrated not according to the traditional Indian lunar calendar, but according to the American work schedule. Several of them have been moved to fixed dates on weekends, just like American holidays. Diwali, the autumn festival of renewal, has been assigned a place within the American end-of-year holiday season. In that case, the Indians say they are learning from the Jewish community, which has had to reinterpret its sacred tradition somewhat in order to respond to the expectations of Christian America. For example, Indo-Americans refer to Diwali as the "Hindu Hanukkah." The American Jewish emphasis on Hanukkah, they point out, has less to do with the traditions of Judaism than with the coincidence that the festival falls near Christmas. American Jews can thus celebrate the holiday season without feeling that they are compromising their special character. And so it is with American Hindus and Diwali.

With this outline of Hinduism as it is practiced in Tampa in mind, it will be possible to trace the development of an Indian community in this southern city and to analyze the impact of a non-Christian outlook on the urban New South.

Indians began coming to Tampa in the early 1970s. They never formed a geographically cohesive unit, but a sense of community emerged nonetheless when a group of pioneers got together to import Indian groceries, clothes, and records. A network of small specialty shops still connects the spatially dispersed community. At first, religious life for Tampa's Indians was restricted to home shrines maintained by the force of familial piety, while samskaras were performed by itinerant priests. Over time, however, more formal institutions developed, culminating in an organizational effort to build a permanent temple and community center as a focus for the group's religious and social life.

Tampa's Indians are eager participants in the Mayor's Interfaith Prayer Brunch, in the planning for official celebrations of Martin Luther King Day, and in various projects sponsored by the National Conference of Christians and Jews. Nevertheless, they are equally eager to maintain their own institutions and organizations so that their special traditions are not too watered down. The Tampa Bay area has more than a dozen Indian community organizations, of which the following are examples:

1. The Indo-American Association (IAA) of Tampa Bay was founded in 1988. It is essentially a secular political action group, but as it sees religious identification as central to its mission, it sponsors community celebrations of Diwali and other sacred festivals, provides reli-

gious education programs, and engages in organized charitable works. The youth division of IAA is the Association of Students of Indo-Americans (ASIA).

2. The Hindu Temple of Florida, Inc. (HTF), is the chief organizational body for the temple/community center, which is scheduled for completion in 1995. Land has already been purchased and consecrated, and there is general agreement that the temple will be an "American" rather than an Indian edifice. That is, it will emphasize open, multipurpose space for congregational worship as well as for secular activities rather than a multitude of small shrines for private devotion and meditation. Moreover, the temple is run by a lay board of directors that, as an additional American innovation, includes several women. The board has opted for a broad-based public fundraising drive in lieu of a traditional process of tithing members. The HTF also sponsors a weekly education program on various aspects of the Sanatana Dharma. Although open to the general public, its targeted audience is composed of those same upscale religious-but-not-observant types discussed above. The HTF also works closely with ASIA in drawing newly arrived university students from India into the life of the local community.

3. The Vishwa Hindu Parishad (VHP, "World Hindu Union") was founded in Bombay in 1965 with the aim of advancing the cause of Hindus both in India and in the diaspora. It has come to be identified with the militant Hindu fundamentalism currently sweeping India, but its role in the United States is more benign. (American Hindus, in fact, scoff at the very notion of Hindu fundamentalism, preferring to emphasize the broad, inclusive, endlessly tolerant nature of their religious tradition.) The main activity of the Florida branch is the development of the Hindu University of America, which seeks to use modern scientific methods in the study of the sacred disciplines and to use religious insights into ethical behavior as the basis of scientific inquiry. Its models are the Catholic University of America in Washington, D.C., and Yeshiva University in New York. It is currently in the planning stage and a development campaign is in the works.

Indo-Americans in Tampa have some specific public policy concerns despite their eagerness to assimilate. Although no Indian is yet in either an elective or appointive office that would allow for a direct policy voice, Indians feel that the affluence and favored status of their community commend them to the attention of policy makers. They want to make sure that lingering Bible Belt attitudes do not lead Tampa's power brokers into taking the "Christian" nature of their culture too much for granted. Specific issues that the Indians seek to inject into the public discourse include the following:

1. Social studies textbooks currently in use tend to present a stereotypical and generally negative image of Asia as a whole and of India in particular. IAA and ASIA are both busily lobbying the various school boards in the metropolitan area to adopt more culturally sensitive texts.

2. There is a long-standing southern tradition, adhered to fervently in Tampa, of introducing just about every public event with a prayer. Indians want to make sure that the ecumenism of the Mayor's Interfaith Prayer Brunch is carried over to a wider array of activities, including the sporting events so dear to the southern heart. They would, for example, love to hear a pandit give the invocation at the Annual Tampa Athletic Circle awards banquet.

3. The Indians have already persuaded the mayor of Tampa to issue an official proclamation heralding Diwali every year. They want to go further, however, and make sure that all enterprises, in both the public and private sectors, recognize Diwali and other major festivals as legitimate "days off." They want to make sure that Hindu students in public schools (including the university) are not penalized for missing days for religious observance. They also want to make sure that there is more public education about the meaning and significance of Hindu festivals.

4. The Indian community remains loyal to its network of small specialty retail shops, but people would also like the convenience of buying Indian foods and other items at their neighborhood Publix or Eckerd and not have to drive all over the city. They are annoyed that Tampa's mainstream merchants have been so slow to recognize the presence of a growing and affluent set of consumers.

5. Above all, however, Indians are deeply concerned about health care. Although a great many Indians are health care professionals, they feel that the special interests of Hindus are not treated respectfully in the city's health care institutions. Hindus, they point out, have special sensitivities regarding such matters as intrusive medical procedures, family visitation, extraordinary life-saving measures, diet, and the treatment of the dead. They are therefore disturbed that the validity of the Hindu point of view is so rarely recognized in the hospital or clinical setting. They wonder why Hindu clergy are not automatically accorded the same

staff privileges as chaplains of other faiths. They also point out that California requires all social workers, psychotherapists, and counselors who work in hospitals to include cross-cultural sensitivity training in their preparation for certification, and they ask why Florida cannot do the same.

These issues are secular as well as explicitly religious. Nevertheless, in all these matters the Indians base their stand on Hindu tradition, which leads them to favor integrative toleration and gradual persuasion rather than aggressive confrontation as a method of public discourse. Indeed, Indians see that tradition as one means of softening some of the harsher aspects of American public discourse.

Indo-Americans are rapidly assimilating, but they do not yet wish to be completely lost in the melting pot. Adherence to religious tradition—albeit not to the multitudinous details of the orthodox faith—is one way they can assert their uniqueness and make a contribution to the evolution of the New South, which they see as needing to move in the direction of a multivocalic urban polity that overcomes its monolithic Bible Belt past.

Women in Congregations

Valerie Fennell

The association between family and religious values in the southern United States may be not only a reflection of the effect of patriarchy in all the South's institutions but also a reflection of changes in U.S. men's and women's roles in the twentieth century. Similar shifts in gender roles occur in other changing societies (Bourguignon 1979:319–20). In "The Cult of Womanhood, 1830–1860," Welter (1966) noted that U.S. men in the nineteenth century became materialists working such long hours that they could not keep the religious traditions of their forebears for want of time to do so. Instead, they turned these duties over to their wives or other women in their families. While men served as leaders for both religion and family institutions, females did more than males to enculturate and reinforce the traditions of both.

While certainly this shift cast on these patriarchal women the responsibilities of perpetuating men's values among themselves and in their homes and churches, it also offered opportunities for women to bring their own interpretations into these settings that did not always agree with those of their men. Sapiro noted, "The impact of women who express the social implications of their religious concerns through organized activities is immeasurable. The number of people who have been fed, clothed, housed, educated, and otherwise comforted by religious organizations of women is uncountable. Through these organizations women have pressed social and political concerns at all ends of the political spectrum and all levels of politics" (1990:170).

Analytically trying to sort out women's and men's values makes it apparent that these are by no means mutually exclusive (Strathern 1981), but an association with work and concerns allocated to the genders exists. Southern men find their concerns with the public realm, where jobs bring wealth and competition offers prestige and esteem, of greater importance when cast into competition with familial and religious concerns, which are women's domains. Allocation of public wealth and resources in southern communities shows the imprint of men's valuing; certainly men control these through bureaucratic organization.

Since women cooperate and work to further concerns in their action domains of family and religion, it is not surprising that they often press for public resources to support these concerns in their communities. Men do not usually directly say that religious and familial concerns are not as important; they merely deem these concerns as not appropriate for public action (Fennell 1989:145). Men instead see these concerns as private, worthy of voluntary support but not of bureaucratic allocations from community taxes. Since public work requires so much energy and attention from everyone, family and religious endeavors can only grow in people's left-over times and energies. And then, only when those who do it are strongly motivated by a sense of role responsibilities, as women often are and men sometimes are. If women are supposed to assume responsibility for family and religious values, men are cast into opposition with these by the culture's contradictory values about masculinity. Wishing to be masculine ordinarily involves southern men in its demonstration through excessive drinking, sexual escapades with women (some of which should be illicit), brawling and fighting with other men, and gambling (Peacock 1971:108–13; Fennell 1989:141), all of which are done with competitiveness with other men in mind. Winning out over other men is considered essential in gathering prestige and esteem from other men and for self-approval.

These behaviors that men consider vital for demonstration of their masculinity are usually discouraged in religious settings, where submissiveness to "God" (the masculine supernatural being that is focal in southern religions) is valued along with attention to familial responsibilities and fidelity to one's spouse. Charitable concern for other families and their children is also admired, as is concern for less fortunate persons. In these endeavors, cooperation is encouraged, though competition may be used to energize fundraising and other kinds of charitable activities.

In the southern town in which I did fieldwork in 1972–73, all these gender issues of religious settings were present. Located at the estuary of a river, this southern county seat thrived on its public bureaucratic activities as well as its riverine and coastal fishing resources. Recreational activities, fishing, tourism, services for a growing retired population, a nearby city, a military shipping port, and a nuclear power plant provided jobs for local people. Curlew Point (a fictional name for the town) had about 3,900 people. The community supported fourteen different Christian congregations, thirteen Protestant and one Roman Catholic. Jewish residents attended religious services in the larger city nearby. Of the local Christian churches, four congregations were African American, and nine were Euro-American. Racial segregation customs were being questioned at the time (those based on age and gender were not), but many persons continued to follow established habits that required segregation in religious organizations. There were situations when the two social races gathered together in the segregated past. These situations were life-cycle events of persons important to a family; attendance was required to show respect despite differences in social race. In such times, mutual respect was expected and shown in this way between Euro-American and African American families.

Only one contemporary congregation included members of both social races. This congregation had grown from intense prayer meetings held in private homes by middle-class persons of established Protestant congregations. Their intensity set them off as part of the movement they called "charismatic" (and some social researchers have called "neo-pentacostalism"), and it led to their leaving their diverse congregations and establishing a new fundamentalist Protestant church.

Pentacostalism (characterized by religious fervor shown in various customs, including "speaking in tongues" and healing by the "laying on of hands") was well established in the community before this time, but the contemporary congregations were racially segregated (as in the past) and working class. There was little sociability between this new church and the fundamentalist congregations established at the beginning of the century (Fennell 1974:182–83). Some elder women, in fact, reported that their congregations all showed much more public religious fervor when they were children around the turn of the century. Religious observance had become far more subdued in their churches in contemporary times. This new fundamentalist movement may well have been Curlew Point's version of a revitalization movement among the middle classes. Certainly generational stresses within the families were apparent to everyone in the community at the time.

In all the churches women and men organized separately for sociability and carrying out work roles. Men assumed roles at the higher ranks that held more organizational authority and received more recognition. These included minister, deacon (and comparable positions), director of Sunday school, and usher. Excepting the position of minister and occasionally a secretary, these church positions were voluntary services provided by congregation members. The minister position often represented the bureaucratic extension of national and regionally organized religious bureaucracies.

Only men were ministers, and it was always preferable even in voluntary church work to have a man in a leadership position over any group of women who might then do the primary work of any particular project. Masculinity was associated with leadership, and the higher the rank the more likely men were to assume the position. Men were also sought as ritual leaders and speakers at ceremonial gatherings; a woman was not as valued in such activities. In addition, activities in which women led were not considered as prestigious.

Projects considered important for women to do for their congregations included any activities involving infants and young children. Women also were expected to organize activities involving food preparation and presentation. Both African American and Euro-American congregations seemed to share these assumptions. These assumptions, of course, parallel women's roles in the familial setting.

Sometimes women were organizers of music for the Euro-American congregations (if men could not be found to do it), playing piano or organ. If drums or guitar were part of services, as with some Euro-American fundamentalist congregations, then men usually were the musicians. In one church the children's bell choir consisted of female children and was directed by a woman who recalled that in Great Britain, where she acquired the bells, it was a man's traditional hobby.

African American church tradition in Curlew Point involved both men and women in choir performance, having both men's and women's choirs, sometimes more than one at a single church. Choir competitions were held as well, and members prided themselves on their performances. Occasionally they argued about which was the best. Both African American and Euro-American congregations had gender-mixed choirs, but women outnumbered the men in the Euro-American churches.

In Curlew Point, Euro-American men often discouraged one another from entering into singing and dancing activities, seeing these endeavors as somehow incompatible with their sense of masculinity, but they spoke pridefully about women in their families who took interest in these. Interestingly, at a national level Euro-American men receive far more attention than Euro-American women for their musical performance abilities. Euro-American men in Curlew Point seemed uneasy with any public emotional displays except those expressing toughness, anger, or humorous poses. Local African American men showed by their frequent involvement in choir activities that they did not share these particular sentiments about masculinity. African American men expressed a full range of emotional displays in musical performance, as did women.

Fundraising activities created the financial base for the congregations and involved everyone in various ways. Euro-American congregations depended heavily on their women's organizations to lead in fundraising activities, including take-out suppers and bazaars (selling handcrafted items). African American congregations held men's and women's "rally" days and competed to see who could raise more for their churches.

In Euro-American congregations Sunday money collection plates were coordinated by men ushers. Both women and men were ushers performing this task in African American congregations. In all churches the financial affairs primarily involved a board (called by various terms) that consisted largely of men along with pastors. As noted above, women were vital in the acquisition of funds for the church, but men usually decided how the money would be spent. Masculinity was strongly linked with the control of money and other forms of wealth. This arrangement reflected familial gender arrangements as well.

Congregations in Curlew Point usually included about twice as many females as males in the adult age groups, from adolescence to old age. Approximately equal numbers of girls and boys attended services. This composition in congregations suggests there may be more in Protestant Christian practice that invites women, less that invites men.

This pattern of diminished male attendance in later life stages is much less pronounced in the Roman Catholic congregation, though even in Roman Catholic congregations women are still more renowned for their religious fervor than men. The Protestant ethic seems to demand a self-reliance that is more pronouncedly unforgiving of failure, and Protestant masculinity ideals offer little place for forgiveness when these are not met. Nor does Protestantism easily allow forgiveness for failure of religious ideals that often stand in opposition to masculine ideals.

Protestant males may have confusion in dealing with the contradictory demands of religious expression and masculinity (Peacock 1971: 109). Success at one casts doubt on the other. And religious forgiveness requires public displays of intense emotional expressions in the ritual conversion process (being moved or touched by the Holy Spirit in a "born again experience" in front of the congregation).

Roman Catholicism institutionalizes community forgiveness through the priest in the ritual of the confessional. Young Catholic males may not feel as much conflict between religious and masculinity ideals. And the excesses of masculinity are readily forgiven in a relatively private religious ritual. The Protestant man must seek the highly public conversion experience in order to have forgiveness for "the excesses of masculinity."

The absence of adult males from congregations was most pronounced at adolescence and young adulthood. Most congregations sought out assertive young married men to be models for adolescent males in the hope they could understand the younger males and reach out to them in ways that would bring them back into attendance. Devout women often spoke about their wish to bring the men of their families "back to God," back to religious participation.

Young men who returned to the church to please a young woman demonstrated their heterosexual virility in acquiescing to her wishes as part of the courtship process. In this context a young man could be both religious and masculine selectively. When a young man's friends asked why he returned to church, they easily understood the wish for the sexual alliance and saw it as motivating the religiosity. Older men who returned to please a wife found much support from the congregation but may well have displeased some men friends who emphasized toughness and independence (their marriages offered public proof of their heterosexuality) as a large component of their masculinity and sense of self.

Women were much admired when they convinced men of their families to participate in religious activities. But it was also commonplace for a woman to participate regularly without her husband or men of her family, sometimes for a lifetime. Women were far more active in seeking conversion experiences in Protestant churches. Men spoke out in congregations more, both "witnessing" spontaneously (standing to tell stories about their religious commitment and the various ways they displayed it with others) and presenting prayers to the supernatural on behalf of the congregation (often at the request of the minister).

Each church had within itself a number of organizations, some for women, some for men. Those for women, however, outnumbered those for men. All were crucial in providing sociability for their members, but each gave itself goals and searched for ways to support the church and its activities as well. These organizations emerged as powerful teams for planning and carrying out the necessary tasks for major fundraising events. They also served as links to other women's organizations outside the church.

Typically the members of one church organization also either belonged to other groups or knew good friends or acquaintances who did, creating powerful overlapping social networks. When larger organizational efforts were required, help was asked of the other organizations. Both African American and Euro-American women had nondenominational organizations of Christian women (Eastern Star, Daughters of the King) to which they belonged in addition to maintaining membership in their congregations.

The Women's Club, the Junior Women's Club, and the Jaycettes were prevailingly Euro-American in their membership, and women who belonged also participated in congregations. All showed an interest in assisting the town's schools (the primary and middle schools) and the hospital and nursing home. All were traditionally involved in creating holiday celebrations within the hospital and the nursing home, as were the religious women's groups.

The primary-school principal, a local positional leader in the county educational bureaucracy, had favored teachers making informal requests of children's mothers to assist in supporting holiday celebrations. With this arrangement he did not have to deal with an organized group of parents. Women new to the town, accustomed to parents' organizations, were suspicious of this, and organized a parents' organization who began to take over some of these functions and also began a dialogue on school policies of various sorts. Women discussed the creation of the parents' organization in all their various groups, including the religious clubs, reporting the date of the first meeting and who was running for office. At religious club meetings of elder women, members remarked on these activities being initiated by the younger women. Women thus were elected to officer positions of the parents' organization. Many younger women speculated that power sharing between the educational bureaucratic leaders and their leaders would ensue.

This same cadre of younger mothers petitioned local churches for space and support for creating children's organizations that were linked to national organizations such as the Girl Scouts, Boy Scouts, and Camp Fire Girls. They also supported summertime children's sports leagues and a small city recreational center. They created local organizations with places for their own children and for the children of other families in the community whose mothers and fathers lacked the time and sense of empowerment to demand these. Many of the churches responded, especially when one of the women turned up as a congregational participant along with other family members. Congregational members often filled the ranks of volunteers for these organizations.

Elder women's religious organizations had particular interests in the perpetuation of the local hospital and nursing home as many of them had relatives, or their friends had relatives, who regularly needed these services. When the county bureaucratic political organization presented policies that advocated building a county hospital elsewhere, taking financial support away from the local Curlew Point hospital, women's organizations, including the religious clubs, quietly and publicly began a voluntary effort to help the hospital stay open.

The county public welfare programs also often suffered from lack of adequate funding for seniors' programs and poor family programs. When this happened, the social workers on staff knew that on some projects they could request that women's voluntary organizations help them through services or financial contributions. Other projects that women's groups helped included charitable campaigns, town beautification projects, upkeep of the pre-Revolution cemetery, and the county library located in Curlew Point.

When bureaucratic funding was inadequate, women's organizations emerged as crucial for keeping many services for the community. Women's religious organizations usually were part of these efforts to keep services that improved the quality of life for the whole community. While men's groups were also involved in some of these efforts, men's groups were more often involved in projects that improved business

and professional conditions for private and public bureaucracies that included them as leaders and workers. These included political support
for development of local resources by corporations and the annual week-
long July 4 celebration, which involved beauty contests, boat races,
fireworks, and military hardware displays, all held to attract tourists
who improved the profitability of businesses.

In the divisions that set economics and politics in men's domains
and family and religion in women's domains, it is clear that the secular
realms had increased importance to men. In Curlew Point the secular bureaucracies controlled economic and political power and wealth.
Religious bureaucracies on the local scene had minimal access to wealth
and most of it was provided through charitable contribution created
through women's group activities in congregations.

While women controlled little wealth and no bureaucracies, they did
manage to create projects that improved the quality of family life for
poorer families and improved the quality of community life for everyone. In their activities women went to the men of their families and
asked for their assistance, reminding their husbands, fathers, sons, and
brothers of the importance of cooperating to improve community life as
well as making profit from it. They also cajoled ministers, principals,
politicians, and employers into contributing and assisting in these community projects. These efforts were viewed as the best possible feminine
endeavors, and men publicly praised women who involved themselves
in these religious activities on behalf of family and community.

Rising Out of the Ashes:
An Exploration of One Congregation's
Use of Southern Symbolism

Scott Lee Thumma

What does it mean to be a southern congregation? For years scholarly and literary analyses have portrayed southern religion as the homogeneous amalgamation of racial segregation, abject poverty, ruralism, and emotional evangelicalism characteristic of the backward Bible Belt (Harrell 1985:45; Reed 1982:123). After a brief sketch of the changing roles of religion and regional identity, I describe one successful congregation in Atlanta that offers a distinctively different perspective on the relationship between southern culture and southern religion. This example portrays the nuanced, multifaceted, and intentional ways modern urban religious groups in the South both may employ and be influenced by the rich heritage and cultural norms of the region.

RELIGION IN THE SOUTH

Numerous scholars during the last twenty-five years have challenged the "Elmer Gantry" image of southern religion. Several of these studies have demonstrated the diversity of styles and complexity of expression within the perceived uniform southern religious experience (Flynt 1985; Gaustad 1985; Harrell 1985). Even in this diversified micro-level picture of southern religious life, however, the various Baptist and Methodist denominations continue to dominate this region (Marty 1985; Roof and McKinney 1987). Current statistical data about religious practices indicate that people who attend churches in the South from any denomination are consistently more active attenders, give more money,

149

and are more conservative in theological beliefs and social issues than people outside the South (Roof and McKinney 1987; Stump 1986:216). These facts point toward the continued existence of a distinctive southern religiosity, a popular southern Protestantism, which, even though not monolithic, still sets the region apart from the rest of the country.

At the same time, other research has suggested that many regional distinctions in religion and society are diminishing in favor of a more generic national culture. The effects of migration both out of and into the southern region have prompted some scholars to argue for a "Southernization of American religion" (Shibley 1991) and an "Americanization of Southern religion" (Egerton 1974; Wells 1987). Along with staggering figures on population change as a result of migration, Shibley offers other data showing traditional southern religions as growing fastest outside the South. "Southern-style evangelicalism" within the region, however, did not keep pace with the rising population during the seventies (Shibley 1991:164). These facts, along with the pluralistic influences of increasing urbanization, indicate that a hegemonic southern religious culture may be weakening, particularly within the growing multicultural cities and urban areas.

Given these findings, it is evident that a tension exists within the religious life of the South. As the region undergoes radical social alterations, the character of southern religion in individual congregations, even if it remains predominantly Baptist and Methodist in denominational affiliation, begins to shift as well. Samuel Hill Jr., noting these changes taking place all over the South, commented that "deeply entrenched attitudes are being shaken, traditional patterns of social life are gradually giving way and being replaced by new" (1966:7). Hill highlighted this tension in southern religion by stating that "the South is no monolith . . . but a regional church exists" (21). A regional church does still exist, but would its now-deceased relatives recognize it? How does the changing cultural and regional context influence the practices within these southern churches? Conversely, how are these New South congregations shaping and reconstructing the regional myths and cultures with which they interact?

REWORKING REGIONAL IDENTITY

In this changing reality of southern urban and suburban life, an argument can be made that soon the acceptance of, or adherence to, a southern regional identity will require an intentional effort of self-definition. A considerable number of sources (Hammond 1988; Roof and McKinney 1987; Wuthnow 1988) suggest that ascriptive identities—those one is born into such as ethnic, familial, and regional characteristics—are weakening in our fragmented, mobile, and pluralistic modern society. Increasingly, to be a southerner will mean to adopt the label and characterization through a process of conscious and intentional choice (Marty 1985:14–15; Reed 1983:31–53). A regional ascriptive identity becomes transformed into an achieved identity. As this happens, the substance of that identity loses its formative ties to the traditional culture. The identity becomes open to constructive and intentional revision in order to fit a shifting cultural context. This malleable regional identity may function not only at the individual level but also at the organizational, societal, and cultural levels. This new regional identity must encompass a distinctively southern image capable of uniting the rich symbolic heritage of the Old South with the modern progressive vision embodied in the New South.

This process can be seen clearly in the history of Atlanta, the premier city of the New South. Throughout its history of public relations campaigns—in 1887 at the Piedmont Exposition, in the "Forward Atlanta" emphases of the 1920s and the 1960s, in the selling of the city to the Olympic Organizing Committee, and now in developing its marketing package to the world for the 1996 Olympics—Atlanta constantly has reinterpreted and promoted its distinctive southern style and heritage in an intentionally modern revisionist manner. Its adoption of the phoenix in 1887 as the city's symbol can be seen as an attempt at both wishful thinking and skillful marketing for a town hardly risen from its Civil War defeat.

Throughout the refinement of its image, Atlanta has been able to retain not only the perception of itself as a distinctively southern city but also as a city with more than just a regional demeanor. Its New South regional identity is a sanitized and modernized version of its former image. The regionalism of Atlanta, and the New South in general, includes the image of a "brave and beautiful" place where residents are "too busy to hate." Atlanta epitomizes the intentional reclamation of traditional cultural themes of the Old South combined with substantial revision and sanitization of its negative elements within a New South regional identity (Reed 1983:31–32).

ONE CONGREGATION'S STORY

The religious life of the region is filled with examples of churches with a distinctive Old South regional character. Instead, I would like to describe one successful religious effort at incorporating Atlanta's New South culture and symbolism into its ethos. This example is the Cathedral of the Holy Spirit (formerly called Chapel Hill Harvester Church) and its senior minister, Bishop Earl Paulk. The church, under Paulk's guidance, consciously has shifted its regional persona to utilize both the symbols and rhetoric of Atlanta and the New South in an effort to become a prominent religious player in the city and nation. This example demonstrates the complex and fluid interaction between regional context and religious expression. The story of the church also shows how regional symbols can be manipulated to restructure a congregation's ethos.

The Cathedral of the Holy Spirit is an independent, nondenominational congregation located in a southeastern suburb of Atlanta. Many of the church's structural features are similar to other large suburban congregations. A majority of its members are young (approximately thirty-five years of age), middle-class, and have a higher than average level of education. The church's theology resonates with the individualistic, entrepreneurial, and expressive themes in American society. One unique feature is that its current racial makeup is composed of 30 percent Caucasian, 65 percent African American, and 5 percent other ethnic groups.

In 1991 the cathedral had a Sunday attendance of 7,500, making it one of the ten largest Protestant congregations in the United States. During 1992, however, Paulk's charismatic authority, as well as the church's size and scope of ministry, eroded under a flood of allegations of considerable sexual misconduct and abuse of authority. The church lost over half of its members and approximately one hundred thousand dollars per week in revenue. This rapid turn of events is the result of a complex variety of factors, including the church's organizational structure, an economic downturn, and even perhaps certain regional variables. In turning to the question of regional influence, then, it is necessary to begin with a sketch of the early history of both Earl Paulk and the church.

Paulk grew up as the son of a very prominent minister and denominational leader of the Church of God in Cleveland, Tennessee. Paulk's family lived in every state in the Deep South before he graduated from high school. Paulk was clearly influenced by rural, lower middle-class southern culture. At the age of seventeen, Paulk was ordained as a minister. Directly after seminary he was sent to Atlanta as the pastor of one of the denomination's largest churches. In 1960, after eight years of service, a sexual indiscretion ended his career with the Church of God. He fled to Phoenix, Arizona, devastated and humiliated until he received an empowering vision from God telling him to return to Atlanta, the place of his former defeat. His mission was to begin an independent ministry focused on providing refuge to the outcast and unwanted members of society.

During its first twelve years, from 1960 to 1972, this ministry struggled to survive. The church's identity centered around Paulk's fall. The similarities between Jesus' death and resurrection, the history of the South and Atlanta in the Civil War, and Paulk's own story were not lost to him or his congregation. Quite often he referred to this theme of rebirth in his sermons. One comment by Paulk exemplifies his reliance on certain Old South themes: "This story may be applied to the history of mankind. It runs in some kind of cycle. From defeat to humility, from humility to exaltation, from exaltation to self-dependence and then back to defeat again." [1]

In 1973 the church and its members joined in the migration of whites from the city into the newly developing suburbs. This period of church history (1973–78) is characterized by an inward focus on the spiritual and familial lives of its members. The southern aspects of the church were downplayed during the seventies, although almost all its members were southern-born. The congregation's homogeneity may account for this lack of explicit regional references. Being southern was a commonly shared, uncontested identity and, therefore, did not need to be stated overtly.

For a variety of reasons the church began to experience tremendous growth from 1979 to 1981. This spectacular growth, a television ministry, and a controversial youth movement created an environment in which the church was viewed with suspicion by Atlanta's religious and civic community. Simultaneously, the church was both growing as an influential congregation and also losing legitimacy in the eyes of many in the city. Likewise, the congregation's accepted heritage of southern traditionalism was weakening with the rapid influx of new members from other regions of the country. The church's organizational structures were undergoing chaotic changes due to the growth. The former identity of the church was shattered. Measures had to be taken to unify the congregation, legitimate the church's ministry, and re-create a stable, grounded identity. One of the ways in which Paulk responded to these problems was to forge a symbolic linkage with the city of Atlanta and a New South regionalism.

ATLANTA AS FERTILE SYMBOLIC GROUND

In the middle of this institutional tumult, Paulk began his intentional appropriation of Atlanta symbolism in a 1982 sermon entitled "Will Atlanta Burn Again?" As in the following quote, Paulk often connected the history of Atlanta, and its symbolic representation of the phoenix, with his own story of defeat and current phenomenal success. "This ministry was started out of a devastation, a heartbreak, and like a phoenix, rising out of the ashes . . . God says I can build out of brokenness." Editions of the church's newspaper began to employ silhouettes of the city's skyline in order to symbolize this connection.

Not long after this sermon church leaders announced that a national conference, called "Atlanta 82," would be held. The practice of using "Atlanta" in conference titles continued through 1988. The symbol used to advertise that conference combined the phoenix and the city's skyline. This symbol was used frequently in both church and local newspapers.

None of these symbols were explicitly interpreted as having any overt religious connotation. It seems apparent that these images were not meant to function as personal religious images but as corporate ones. They also provided a symbolic link with the prosperity and national recognition of the city of Atlanta. In 1982, Atlanta was judged as the number one place to live in the United States and from 1980 to 1986 it was the third fastest-growing metropolitan area in the nation (Helyar 1988:1). At the same time, Paulk's church was among the fastest-growing churches in the country.

The church's image problem improved greatly during these years, so much so that Paulk labeled 1985 as "The Year of Credibility." The church gained considerable notability, political influence, and respectability in the state, the nation, and even globally. The final time the phoenix was used by the church an attempt was made to portray a global perspective. This image was used only once, in early 1985. From that point on the symbol of the phoenix was never again used in any church literature.

By 1985 Chapel Hill Harvester had grown to approximately 3,500 members and a budget of $5 million. Paulk met with President Reagan and Senator Nunn in Washington that year. With such a large voting constituency under his leadership, he also had the attention of state and local politicians. His television program was broadcast throughout the United States and in seven other countries. At the same time, the church was experiencing another tremendous influx of members. This time it was composed of middle-class African Americans. Paulk could optimistically comment, early in 1985, about both the future of the church and the city: "Atlanta will become the religious center of the world. Atlanta became a symbol of victory over defeat. The phoenix that rises out of the dust of defeat, that lifts its head in pride and says, 'God is not done with Atlanta yet!' It is becoming one of the revival centers of the world."

By 1987, with the continued influx of blacks, Paulk was pastoring one of the largest groupings of African Americans in the city. Weekly attendance averaged nearly five thousand and the yearly income approached $6.5 million. The church provided a sizable power base for Paulk. His comments were no longer in the future tense (as in the previous quote), but in the present tense and full of certainty. "Atlanta is the spiritual capital of the world," he would often exclaim. Around this time he began to rely heavily on the symbolism of black liberation, civil rights, and the legacy of Martin Luther King Jr. "We are the new way . . . we are the (MLK) dream fulfilled." Clearly Chapel Hill Harvester Church had overcome its identity problems; it no longer needed any external validation.

THE VARIETY OF REGIONAL INFLUENCES

This brief historical sketch highlights the complex and multidimensional influence of regional myths and symbols throughout the life of this congregation. Early in Paulk's life the southern regional influences shaped his ideals, mannerisms, preaching style, and worldview. Then, after Paulk left the Church of God, the southern myth of the lost cause joined with Atlanta's embodiment of this myth in the phoenix to become a central image of the congregation. This aspect of southern identity, of rising from defeat, functioned as a vital totemic symbol to weld a group consciousness and promote unity. Ideologically, it informed Paulk's interpretation of his own fall and past failures. It also shaped the theological mission of the church as "a refuge to fallen and hurting people." This image gave meaning to the most chaotic period of the church's history, both explaining the turmoil and reconnecting it to a regional myth. The phoenix further functioned as a form of self-fulfilling prophecy. It identified the church's ideals and goals as it helped the congregation live up to them. The phoenix proved to be a powerful motivational tool that symbolized the possibility of becoming the "beautiful bird" of the myth. When the church actually became successful, the symbol was discarded. The image was no longer necessary because, in a very real way, the church had embodied the myth.

When the church held no status with the city's elite, Paulk's prophetic pronouncements about the city becoming the spiritual capital of the world forged an ideological linkage between the city and his own success. In his comments such as "Oh Atlanta, Atlanta . . ."—reminiscent of Jesus' prayer over Jerusalem—Paulk both denigrated those who were attacking him and also portrayed himself as their savior weeping over their ignorance at persecuting him.

Once the church became prosperous, Paulk shifted his symbolic connections with the city. He switched from being the city's suffering savior to its prophetic judge, chastising elected officials and attempting to direct the city's policies. Paulk's interaction with the city changed from efforts of legitimating the ministry of the church to efforts of maintaining his authority, increasing the congregation's prestige, and extending the scope of his social agenda.

A NEW "OLD SOUTH" CONGREGATION

Paulk's current use of southern rhetoric shows a gradually increasing emphasis on a progressive New South identity. The combination of Old and New South characteristics has helped Paulk reaffirm a distinctively southern atmosphere that most nonsouthern members find palatable. This regional rhetoric provides both old and new members, especially those dislocated and uprooted from their birthplaces by social forces within a highly mobile society, with a ready-made heritage. Members are offered a grounding in a history, given a sense of place in which to root their families.

Many stereotypical Old South traditions are strongly reinforced. This Charismatic congregation constantly expresses friendliness and southern hospitality. As the bulletin proudly proclaims, "You are never a stranger here" and "You are always loved by our family." Worship services include references to a "sense of place" and the southern heritage of the church with its roots in South Georgia. Paulk's tales of the congregation's history parallel a mythologized, *Gone with the Wind* portrayal of the South. The recently built neo-gothic cathedral features a huge double staircase reminiscent of an antebellum mansion. A distinctive style of dress has been adopted by many of the influential white, and some black, female church members. This dress style, with its long flowing dresses of padded shoulders, low neckline, ample ruffles, and a tight bodice, is characteristic of the typical southern belle with perfect "hour-glass" figure. Finally, Paulk continues to use paternalistic comments, such as "honey" and "little darlings," in his authoritarian preaching style. Each of these features helps to promote a distinctively Old South atmosphere.

At the same time, Paulk avoids other aspects of this traditionalism that could be interpreted as offensive. He never discusses North/South hostilities or the Civil War. He excuses his paternalistic comments humorously by suggesting they are due to "bad habits from a backward childhood." He preaches sermons that promote a minimally egalitarian, modern redefinition of gender roles and responsibilities in the home and workplace. He tempers his authoritarian preaching style with an emphasis on tolerance, love, and servanthood. Paulk forcefully affirms racial integration and ethnic harmony—an integration demonstrated in his congregation. He presents a revised understanding of localism that emphasizes small intentional and intimate communities. He also encourages local social and political activism, yet this localism is tempered by broader national and global perspectives.

Finally, and most important, Paulk and the church fervently assert that religion must play an important role in the total life of the South in general and of Atlanta in particular. The cathedral offers a different vision of what this means. The church's vision not only includes personal salvation and evangelical outreach but also addresses political affairs, economic decisions, and social activism. It is the mission of this amalgamated Old/New South congregation not only to convert southern souls but also to transform southern society.

This essay began with the question of what it means to be a southern congregation, but this essay does not attempt to answer that question definitively. What should be clear, however, is that southern religiosity no longer necessarily implies an evangelical, traditionalist reflection of Old South cultural characteristics. A close look at southern religious life shows the influence of region to be dynamic and diverse. As the South continues to urbanize and "Americanize," this regional identity and its contents will increasingly become an intentional and personal choice made by individuals. Regional influences, especially New South regionalism, on religious phenomena will be open to both negotiation and innovation. Atlanta's identity, history, and symbolism was offered as an explicit example of this New South regionalism. The history of the Cathedral of the Holy Spirit was presented as an example of the complex and subtle interactions between this New South regionalism and traditional southern religious life. Within this narrative, contemporary southern regional religion appears multifaceted, nuanced, and in flux. Nevertheless, it is still recognizably southern.

NOTE

1. This comment by Bishop Paulk and other quotes that follow are all taken from the bishop's sermons.

References

Abu-Lughod, Lila. 1990. The Romance of Resistance: Tracing Transformations of Power Through Bedouin Women. *American Ethnologist* 17:41–55.

Allen, Judson Boyce. 1958. Preaching, Southern Baptist. In *Encyclopedia of Southern Baptists II*, 1108–10. Nashville: Broadman Press.

Ammerman, Nancy Tatom. 1990. *Baptist Battles: Social Change and Religious Conflict in the Southern Baptist Convention*. New Brunswick: Rutgers University Press.

Anderson, Jon. 1992. Bible Belt Catholicism. Unpublished research report, Catholic University of America.

Anglin, Mary K. 1990. "A Lost and Dying World": Women's Labor in the Mica Industry of Southern Appalachia. Ph.D. diss., New School for Social Research.

Angrosino, Michael V. 1983. Religion Among Overseas Indians. In *Main Currents in Indian Sociology*, vol. 5, edited by G. R. Gupta, 357–98. New York: Advent.

Baba Kunle. 1991. Interview by Beatriz Morales, Georgia State University, Atlanta, Ga.

Baer, Hans A. 1984. *The Black Spiritual Movement: A Religious Response to Racism*. Knoxville: University of Tennessee Press.

Baer, Hans A., and Merrill Singer. 1992. *African-American Religion in the Twentieth Century: Varieties of Protest and Accommodation*. Knoxville: University of Tennessee Press.

Barnhart, Joe Edward. 1986. *The Southern Baptist Holy War*. Austin: Texas Monthly Press.

Bartlett, Josiah R., and Laile E. Bartlett. 1990. *A Religion for the "Non-Religious": An Overview of Unitarian Universalism*. Berkeley, Calif.: J. R. and L. E. Bartlett.

Bascom, William. 1972. *Shango in the New World*. Austin: University of Texas at Austin.

Bellah, Robert N. 1967. Civil Religion in America. *Daedalus* (Winter): 1–21.

Bellah, Robert N., Richard Madsen, William M. Sullivan, Ann Swidler, and

Steven M. Tipton. 1985. *Habits of the Heart: Individualism and Commitment in American Life.* New York: Harper and Row.

Billings, Dwight. 1990. Religion as Opposition: A Gramscian Analysis. *American Journal of Sociology* 96:1–31.

Bourdieu, Pierre. 1977. *Outline of a Theory of Practice.* Cambridge: Cambridge University Press.

Bourguignon, Erika. 1979. *Psychological Anthropology.* New York: Holt, Rinehart and Winston.

Brandon, George E. 1991. Racial-Ethnic Identity and Religious Alliance in a Black Nationalist Movement. Panel on Nationalism, Race, and Ethnicity in African-American Religion, American Anthropological Association.

Bulletin of the Catholic Layman's Association of Georgia, 1922–1924. (Savannah) 25 January 1922–23 February 1924.

Bureau of the Census. 1990. *Census of Population and Housing: Summary of Social, Economic and Housing Characteristics, N.C.* Washington, D.C.: U.S. Government Printing Office.

Carnegie, Charles V. 1987. Is Family Land an Institution? *Afro-Caribbean Villages in Historical Perspective. ACIJ Research Review* 2:83–99. Kingston: African-Caribbean Institute of Jamaica.

Cashin, Edward. 1962. Tom Watson and the Catholic Laymen's Association of Georgia. Ph.D. diss., Fordham University.

Chafe, Wallace, and Deborah Tannen. 1987. The Relation Between Written and Spoken Language. *Annual Review of Anthropology* 16:383–407.

Chick, J. T. 1982. *The Godfathers.* Chino, Calif.: Chick.

———. n.d. *Are Roman Catholics Christians?* Chino, Calif.: Chick.

Chiniquy, Charles P. 1886. *Fifty Years in the Church of Rome,* 3d ed. Montreal: W. Drysdale.

Cohen, Sandra. 1973. Two Essays on Ethnic Identity and the Yoruba of Harlem: Essay I: Ethnic Identity in New York City; Essay II: Ethnic Identity in the South. Master's thesis, Columbia University.

Commission on Appraisal. 1989. *The Quality of Religious Life in Unitarian Universalist Congregations.* Boston: Unitarian Universalist Association.

Corbin, David Alan. 1981. *Life, Work, and Rebellion in the Coal Fields: The Southern West Virginia Miners, 1880–1922.* Urbana: University of Illinois Press.

Couto, Richard A. 1993. The Memory of Miners and the Conscience of Capital: Coalminers' Strikes as Free Space. In *Fighting Back in Appalachia: Traditions of Resistance and Change,* edited by Stephen L. Fisher, Philadelphia: Temple University Press.

Crews, Clyde F. 1987. *An American Holy Land.* Wilmington, Del.: Michael Glazier.

Dale, William Pratt. 1958. Alabama Baptist Convention. *Encyclopedia of Southern Baptists I*, 18. Nashville: Broadman Press.

Dawkins, Richard. 1989. Put Your Money on Evolution. *New York Times*, 9 April, sec. 7.

Dawson, Joan. 1991. God, Etc.: Behind the Percentages. *UU News* (Newsletter of the Unitarian Universalist Fellowship of Winston-Salem), July.

Egerton, John. 1974. *The Americanization of Dixie: The Southernization of America*. New York: Harper and Row.

Feeley-Harnik, Gillian. 1981. *The Lord's Table: Eucharist and Passover in Early Christianity*. Philadelphia: University of Pennsylvania Press.

Fennell, Valerie. 1974. Hierarchical Aspects of Age Relations in Curlew Point. Ph.D. diss., University of North Carolina, Chapel Hill.

———. 1981. Friendship and Kinship in Older Women's Organizations: Curlew Point, 1973. In *Dimensions: Aging, Culture and Health*, by Christine L. Fry and contributors, 131–43. New York: Praeger.

———. 1989. Epilogue: Musings on Ethnocentric Sexism in Traditional Ethnographies of the South. In *Women in the South: An Anthropological Perspective*, edited by Holly Mathews, 136–46. Athens: University of Georgia Press.

Fenton, John Y. 1988. *Transplanting Religious Traditions: Asian Indians in America*. New York: Praeger.

Finke, Roger and Rodney Stark. 1992. *The Churching of America, 1776–1990*. New Brunswick: Rutgers University Press.

Fitzpatrick, Vincent. 1989. *H. L. Mencken*. New York: Continuum.

Flynt, Wayne. 1985. One in the Spirit, Many in the Flesh: Southern Evangelicals. In *Varieties of Southern Evangelicalism*, edited by David Edwin Harrell, 23–44. Macon, Ga.: Mercer University Press.

Foner, Eric. 1993. Memo to Bill II: Time for a Third Reconstruction. *The Nation* (February 1): 117–19.

Fordham, Signithia. 1988. Racelessness as a Factor in Black Students' School Success: Pragmatic Strategy or Pyrrhic Victory? *Harvard Educational Review* 58 (1): 54–84.

Gaustad, Edwin S. 1985. Regionalism in American Religion. In *Religion in the South*, edited by Charles R. Wilson, 155–72. Jackson: University Press of Mississippi.

Geisler, Norman L., ed. 1980. *Inerrancy*. Grand Rapids: Zondervan.

Gerlach, Luther P., and Virginia H. Hine. 1970. *People, Power, and Change: Movements of Social Transformation*. Indianapolis: Bobbs-Merrill.

Giardina, Denise. 1989a. Moving Mountains. *Southern Exposure*, Spring, 43–45.

———. 1989b. Solidarity in Appalachia. *The Nation*, July 3, 12–14.

Goffman, Erving. 1961. *Encounters: Two Studies in the Sociology of Inter-action*. Indianapolis: Bobbs-Merrill.

————. 1981. *Forms of Talk*. Philadelphia: University of Pennsylvania Press.

Gould, Stephen Jay. 1983. *Hen's Teeth and Horse's Toes*. New York: Norton.

————. 1991. *Bully for Brontosaurus*. New York: Norton.

————. 1993. *Eight Little Piggies*. New York: Norton.

Greeley, Andrew M. 1977. *An Ugly Little Secret: Anti-Catholicism in North America*. Kansas City: Sheed Andrews and McMeel.

Greenhouse, Carol. 1986. *Praying for Justice*. Ithaca: Cornell University Press.

Griesman, H. C., and Sharon S. Mayers. 1977. The Social Construction of Unreality: The Real American Dilemma. *Dialectical Anthropology* 2:57–67.

Griffin, Sister M. Julian (and Mrs. Gillian Brown). 1979. *Tomorrow Comes the Song: The Story of Catholicism Among the Black Population of South Georgia, 1850–1978*. Savannah: Diocese of Savannah.

Gutman, Herbert G. 1976. *Work, Culture, and Society in Industrializing America: Essays on American Working-Class and Social History*. New York: Vintage Books.

Haley, Alex, and David Stevens. 1993. *Queen: The Story of an American Family*. New York: William Morrow.

Hammond, Phillip. 1988. Religion and the Persistence of Identity. *Journal for the Scientific Study of Religion* 27 (1): 1–11.

Harding, Susan F. 1987. Convicted by the Holy Spirit: The Rhetoric of Fundamental Baptist Conversion. *American Ethnologist* 14:167–81.

Harper, Burgess. 1931. Sketch of the Life and Administration of Rev. Burgess Harper: For Fifty-One Years a Faithful Minister of the Gospel in Warren, Halifax and Nash Counties, January 10. Manuscript.

Harper Family. 1989. 1989 Family Reunion Document.

————. 1992. Harper Family Newsletter, vol. 1, no. 1 (September 5–6).

Harrell, David Edwin, ed. 1985. The South: Seedbed of Sectarianism. In *Varieties of Southern Evangelicalism*, edited by David Edwin Harrell, 45–57. Macon, Ga.: Mercer University Press.

Helyar, John. 1988. The Big Hustle. *Wall Street Journal*, 29 February.

Herberg, Will. 1960. *Protestant, Catholic, Jew*. Garden City: Doubleday.

Hill, Samuel S., Jr. 1966. *Southern Churches in Crisis*. New York: Holt, Rinehart and Winston.

————. 1972. *Religion and the Solid South*. Nashville: Abingdon Press.

————. 1988. *Varieties of Southern Religious Experience*. Baton Rouge: Louisiana State University Press.

Hobson, Fred. 1987. "This Hellawful South": Mencken and the Late Confederacy. In *Critical Essays on H. L. Mencken*, edited by Douglas C. Stenerson, 174–85. Boston: G. K. Hall.

Holland, Dorothy C, and Joan Valsiner. 1988. Cognition, Symbols, and Vygotsky's Developmental Psychology. *Ethos* 16:247–72.

Hollyday, Joyce. 1989. "Amazing Grace." *Sojourners,* July, 12–22.

Hunt, Carl M. 1979. *Oyotunji Village: The Yoruba Movement in America.* Washington, D.C.: University Press of America.

Hunter, James Davison. 1983. *American Evangelicalism: Conservative Religion and the Quandary of Modernity.* New Brunswick: Rutgers University Press.

———. 1987. *Evangelicalism: The Coming Generation.* Chicago: University of Chicago Press.

Jacobs, Claude, and Andrew J. Kaslow. 1991. *The Spiritual Churches of New Orleans: Origins, Beliefs, and Rituals of an African-American Religion.* Knoxville: University of Tennessee Press.

Jensen, Joan M. 1988. *Passage from India: Asian Indian Immigrants in North America.* New Haven: Yale University Press.

Jones, Yvonne V. 1980. Kinship Affiliation Through Time: Black Homecomings and Family Reunions in a North Carolina County. *Ethnohistory* 27 (1): 49–66.

Katz, Nathan. 1991. *Tampa Bay's Asian-Origin Religious Communities.* Tampa, Fla.: National Conference of Christians and Jews.

Kelber, Werner H. 1983. *The Oral and the Written Gospel.* Philadelphia: Fortress Press.

Knowlton, David C. 1992. No One Can Serve Two Masters or Native Anthropologist as Oxymoron. *International Journal of Moral and Social Studies* 7 (1): 72–88.

Kosmin, Barry A. 1991. *Research Report: The National Survey of Religious Identification 1989–1990 (Selected Tabulations).* New York: Graduate School and University Center, City University of New York.

Lanman, Charles. 1849. *Letters from the Allegheny Mountains.* New York: Putnam.

Levine, Lawrence. 1977. *Black Culture and Black Consciousness.* New York: Oxford University Press.

Levi-Strauss, Claude. 1966. *The Savage Mind.* Chicago: University of Chicago Press.

Lockley, Edith A. 1936. Spiritualist Scct in Nashville. Master's thesis, Fisk University.

Manchester, William. 1983. *Disturber of the Peace: The Life of H. L. Mencken.* Amherst: University of Massachusetts Press.

Marable, Manning. 1984. *Race, Reform and Rebellion: The Second Reconstruction in Black America, 1945–1982.* Jackson: University Press of Mississippi.

Marsden, George M. 1980. *Fundamentalism and American Culture.* New York: Oxford University Press.

Marty, Martin. 1985. The Revival of Evangelicalism and Southern Religion. In *Varieties of Southern Evangelicalism,* edited by David Edwin Harrell, 7–22. Macon, Ga.: Mercer University Press.

Mauss, Marcel. 1950. Essai sur les variations saisonnières des sociétés Eskimos. In *Sociologie et Anthropologie,* 389–475. Paris: Presses Universitaires de France.

McDonogh, Gary W. 1987. Ethnicity, Urbanization and Consciousness in Savannah. In *Shades of the Sunbelt: Essays on Ethnicity, Race, and the Urban South,* edited by R. Miller and G. Pozzetta, 53–73. Westport, Conn.: Greenwood Press.

———. 1993. *Black and Catholic in Savannah, Georgia.* Knoxville: University of Tennessee Press.

McNally, Michael. 1987. A Peculiar Institution: A History of the Catholic Parish in the Southeast (1850–1980). In *The American Catholic Parish,* vol. 1, edited by Jay Dolan, 117–234. Mahwah, N.J.: Paulist Press.

McWhiney, Grady. 1988. *Cracker Culture: Celtic Ways in the Old South.* Tuscaloosa: University of Alabama Press.

Mencken, H. L. 1920. *Prejudices: Second Series.* New York: Alfred A. Knopf.

———. 1926. *Prejudices: Fifth Series.* New York: Alfred A. Knopf.

———. 1965. The Monkey Trial: A Reporter's Account. In *D-Days at Dayton: Reflections on the Scopes Trial,* edited by Jerry R. Tompkins, 35–51. Baton Rouge: Louisiana State University Press.

Miller, Randall M., and Jon Wakelyn, eds. 1983. *Catholics in the Old South: Essays on Church and Culture.* Macon, Ga.: Mercer University Press.

Morales, Beatriz. 1990. Afro-Cuban Religious Transformation: A Comparative Study of Lucumi Religion and the Tradition of Spirit Beliefs. Ph.D. diss., City University of New York.

Murphy, Robert F. 1979. *An Overture to Social Anthropology.* Englewood Cliffs, N.J.: Prentice-Hall.

Neville, Gwen Kennedy. 1987. *Kinship and Pilgrimage.* Oxford: Oxford University Press.

Nolan, Charles E. 1987. Modest and Humble Crosses: A History of Catholic Parishes in the South Central Region. In *The American Catholic Parish: A History from 1850 to the Present,* edited by J. P. Dolan, 235–46. New York: Paulist Press.

Numbers, Ronald L. 1992. *The Creationists.* New York: Alfred A. Knopf.

Ochs, Stephen. 1990. *Desegregating the Altar.* Baton Rouge: Louisiana State University Press.

O'Connell, J. J. 1879. *Catholicity in the Carolinas and Georgia.* New York: D. J. Sadlier.

O'Connor, Flannery. 1969. The Catholic Novelist in the Protestant South. In

Mystery and Manners, edited by Sally Fitzgerald and Robert Fitzgerald, 191–209. New York: Farrar, Straus & Giroux.

———. 1979. *The Habit of Being: Letters,* edited by Sally Fitzgerald. New York: Farrar, Straus & Giroux.

Odell Baptist Church. 1978. The Ninety-fifth Anniversary Publication of the Odell Baptist Church, August. Littleton, N.C. Manuscript.

Ong, Walter J. 1969. World as View and World as Event. *American Anthropologist* 71:634–47.

Orsi, Robert A. 1985. *The Madonna of 115 Street: Faith and Community in Italian Harlem, 1880–1950.* New Haven: Yale University Press.

Ortner, Sherry B. 1984. Theory in Anthropology Since the Sixties. *Comparative Studies in Society and History* 1:126–66.

Overton, William R. 1982. Speech to Pennsylvania Appellate Judges. 29 June. Philadelphia.

Packer, James I. 1980. The Adequacy of Human Language. In *Inerrancy,* edited by Norman L. Geisler, 197–228. Grand Rapids: Zondervan.

Parker, Reverend Aaron. 1992. Why a White Jesus Won't Work. Butler Street Baptist Church, Atlanta, Ga., 6 December. Sermon.

Parsons, Paul F. 1987. *Inside America's Christian Schools.* Macon, Ga.: Mercer University Press.

Patterson, W. Morgan. 1971. Baptist Faith and Message. *Encyclopedia of Southern Baptists III,* 1589–94. Nashville: Broadman Press.

Pauck, Wilhelm. 1968. *Harnack and Troeltsch: Two Historical Theologians.* New York: Oxford University Press.

Peacock, James L. 1971. The Southern Protestant Ethic Disease. In *The Not So Solid South,* edited by J. Kenneth Moreland, 108–13. Athens: University of Georgia Press.

Peshkin, Alan. 1986. *God's Choice: The Total World of a Fundamentalist Christian School.* Chicago: University of Chicago Press.

Pleasant Grove Baptist Church. 1986. The One Hundred and Fourth Anniversary of the Pleasant Grove Baptist Church, Hollister, N.C. Manuscript.

Pope, Liston. 1942. *Millhands and Preachers.* New Haven: Yale University Press.

Rappaport, Roy A. 1971. Ritual, Sanctity, and Cybernetics. *American Anthropologist* 73:59–76.

Reed, John Shelton. 1982. *One South: An Ethnic Approach to Regional Culture.* Baton Rouge: Louisiana State University Press.

———. 1983. *Southerners: The Social Psychology of Sectionalism.* Chapel Hill: University of North Carolina Press.

Richardson, Miles. 1990. The Spatial Sense of the Sacred in Spanish America and in the American South. In *By Means of Performance,* edited by Richard

Schechner and Willa Appel, 221–35. Cambridge: Cambridge University Press.

Richardson, Miles, and Robert Dunton. 1989. Culture in Its Places: A Humanistic Presentation. In *The Relevance of Culture,* edited by Morris Freilich, 75–90. New York: Bergin & Garvey.

Ricoeur, Paul. 1979. The Model of the Text: Meaningful Action Considered as a Text. In *Interpretive Social Science,* edited by Paul Rabinow and William M. Sullivan, 73–102. Berkeley: University of California Press.

Roof, Wade Clark, and William McKinney. 1987. *American Mainline Religion: Its Changing Shape and Future.* New Brunswick: Rutgers University Press.

Rose, Susan D. 1988. *Keeping Them Out of the Hands of Satan: Evangelical Schooling in America.* New York: Routledge.

Rosenberg, Ellen M. 1989. *The Southern Baptists: A Subculture in Transition.* Knoxville: University of Tennessee Press.

Ruse, Michael L. 1984. A Philosopher's Day in Court. In *Science and Creationism,* edited by Ashley Montagu, 311–42. New York: Oxford University Press.

Sacks, Karen. 1989. Toward a Unified Theory of Class, Race, and Gender. *American Ethnologist* 16:534–50.

Sahlins, Marshall. 1976. *Culture and Practical Reason.* Chicago: University of Chicago Press.

———. 1981. *Historical Metaphors and Mythical Realities.* Ann Arbor: University of Michigan Press.

Sapiro, Virginia. 1990. *Women in American Society,* 2d ed. Mountain View, Calif.: Mayfield Publishing Co.

Sherzer, Joel. 1987. A Discourse-Centered Approach to Language and Culture. *American Anthropologist* 89:295–309.

Shibley, Mark. 1991. The Southernization of American Religion. *Sociological Analysis* 52 (2): 159–74.

Shurden, Walter B. 1972. *Not a Silent People: Controversies That Have Shaped the Southern Baptists.* Nashville: Broadman Press.

Smout, Kary D. 1991. Terminology Battles: Word Meanings as Rhetorical Tools in the Creation/Evolution Controversy. Ph.D. diss., Duke University.

Stark, Rodney and William Sims Bainbridge. 1985. *The Future of Religion.* Berkeley: University of California Press.

Stewart, Kathleen C. 1990. Speak for Yourself: Gender as Dialogic in Appalachia. In *Uncertain Terms: The Negotiation of Gender in American Culture,* edited by Faye Ginsburg and Anna Tsing. Boston: Beacon Press.

Strathern, Marilyn. 1981. Self Interest and the Social Good. In *Sexual Meanings: The Cultural Construction of Gender and Sexuality,* edited by Sherry

Ortner and Harriet Whitehead, 166–91. Cambridge: Cambridge University Press.

Stromberg, Peter G. 1990. Ideological Language in the Transformation of Identity. *American Anthropologist* 92:42–56.

Stump, Roger W. 1984. Regional Migration and Religious Commitment in the United States. *Journal for the Scientific Study of Religion* 23:292–303.

———. 1986. Regional Variations in the Determinants of Religious Participation. *Review of Religious Research* 27:208–25.

Suleiman, Susan. 1980. Introduction: Varieties of Audience-Oriented Criticism. In *The Reader in the Text: Essays on Audience and Interpretation,* edited by Susan R. Suleiman and Inge Crosman, 3–45. Princeton: Princeton University Press

Takaki, Ronald. 1989. *Strangers from a Different Shore: A History of Asian Americans.* Boston: Little, Brown.

Taub, Richard. 1976. Immigrants from the Indian Subcontinent and the Social Experience of Ethnic Groups in America. In *Indians from the Indian Subcontinent in the U.S.A.,* edited by Hekmat Elkhanialy and Ralph W. Nichols, 19–31. Chicago: India League of America.

Thompson, James J. 1986. *Fleeing the Whore of Babylon: A Modern Conversion Story.* Westminster, Md.: Christian Classics.

Troeltsch, Ernst. 1960 (1931). *The Social Teaching of the Christian Churches,* translated by Olive Wyon. Chicago: University of Chicago Press.

Tyson, Ruel W., James L. Peacock, and Daniel Patterson, eds. 1988. *Diversities of Gifts: Field Studies in Southern Religion.* Urbana: University of Illinois Press.

Urban, Greg, and Joel Sherzer. 1988. The Linguistic Anthropology of Native South America. *Annual Review of Anthropology* 17:283–307.

Wagner, Melinda Bollar. 1990. *God's Schools: Choice and Compromise in American Society.* New Brunswick: Rutgers University Press.

Wallace, Anthony F. C. 1966. *Religion: An Anthropological View.* New York: Random House.

Wamble, Hugh. 1964. Landmarkism: Doctrinaire Ecclesiology Among Baptists. *Church History* 33:429–47.

Watson, Thomas. 1917. *Roman Catholics in America Falsifying History and Poisoning the Minds of Schoolchildren.* Thompson, Ga.: Jeffersonian Publishing Company.

Wells, Alan. 1987. *Mass Media and Society.* Lexington, Mass.: Lexington Books.

Welter, Barbara. 1966. The Cult of True Womanhood, 1830–1860. *American Quarterly* 18:151–74.

Wesley, Alice Blair. 1987. *Myths of Time and History: A Unitarian Universalist Theology*. Privately published.

White, O. Kendall, Jr. 1972. Constituting Norms and the Formal Organization of American Churches. *Sociological Analysis* 33 (2): 95–109.

White, Theodore H. 1961. *The Making of the President 1960*. New York: Atheneum.

Wiggins, William H., Jr. 1987. *O Freedom! Afro-American Emancipation Celebrations*. Knoxville: University of Tennessee Press.

Williams, Brett. 1988. *Upscaling Downtown: Stalled Gentrification in Washington, D.C.* Ithaca: Cornell University Press.

Williams, Raymond Brady. 1988. *Religions of Immigrants from India and Pakistan: New Threads in the American Tapestry*. Cambridge: Cambridge University Press.

Wilson, John. 1978. *Religion in American Society: The Effective Presence*. Englewood Cliffs, N.J.: Prentice-Hall.

Woodward, C. Vann. 1938. *Tom Watson: Agrarian Rebel*. Savannah: Beehive Press.

Wuthnow, Robert. 1988. *The Restructuring of American Religion*. Princeton: Princeton University Press.

———. 1993. *Christianity in the Twenty-first Century: Reflections on the Challenges Ahead*. Oxford: Oxford University Press.

Yancey, Dwayne. 1990. Thunder in the Coalfields: The UMW's Strike Against Pittston. *Roanoke Times & World News,* 29 April.

Yarrow, Michael. 1990. Voices from the Coalfields: How Miners' Families Understand the Crisis of Coal. In *Communities in Economic Crisis: Appalachia and the South,* edited by John Gaventa, Barbara Ellen Smith, and Alex Willingham. Philadelphia: Temple University Press.

Yun, Grace, ed. 1989. *A Look Beyond the Model Minority Image: Critical Issues in Asian America*. New York: Minority Rights Group.

Zimmerman, Blanche Raper. 1982. *New Dimensions of the Spirit: The Story of the Unitarian-Universalists of Winston-Salem*. Winston-Salem: Unitarian Universalist Fellowship of Winston-Salem.

Contributors

JON W. ANDERSON is an associate professor of anthropology at the Catholic University of America in Washington, D.C. He has conducted research in Afghanistan and Pakistan on tribal and traditional Islamic cultures and maintains an active research interest in Middle East studies with an emphasis on changing sites of religious discourse, systems of knowledge, and traditional professionals.

MARY ANGLIN is engaged in postgraduate work in the Medical Anthropology Program at the University of California, San Francisco, and the Department of Epidemiology at the University of California, Berkeley. She is also a visiting scholar at the Beatrice M. Bain Research Group for the Study of Women and Gender, University of California, Berkeley. Her research addresses women's efforts as cancer survivors and how people living with HIV/ AIDS organize around issues of access to health care.

MICHAEL V. ANGROSINO is a professor of anthropology at the University of South Florida. He has conducted research on overseas Indian communities in the Caribbean and the United States. Author of *Documents of Interaction: Biography, Autobiography, and Life History in the Social Sciences,* Angrosino's research interests include the role of religion in modern society, mental health service delivery and policy, and techniques of oral history.

HANS A. BAER is a professor of anthropology at the University of Arkansas at Little Rock. In addition to African American religion, his research interests include Mormonism, medical pluralism in North America and Europe, critical medical anthropology, and social life in East Germany both before and after unification.

ANDREW BILLINGSLEY, chair of the Department of Family and Community Development Studies at the University of Maryland at College Park, is a well-known scholar of the African American family. His most recent book, *Climbing Jacob's Ladder: The Future of African American Families,* continues his challenge to the "tangle of pathology" framework that permeates the study of African American families and communities. He is presently conducting a national study of community outreach programs of African American churches.

VALERIE FENNELL is an associate professor of anthropology at Georgia State University. Both her research and teaching have focused on age and gender relations cross culturally and in the southern United States.

FAYE V. HARRISON is an associate professor in the Department of Anthropology at the University of Tennessee in Knoxville. She is interested in the African diaspora and has done research in Jamaica on local-level politics, gender, informal sector work, and the internationalization of drug trafficking. She edited *Decolonizing Anthropology: Moving Further Toward an Anthropology of Liberation.*

FLEDA MASK JACKSON is Director of the Historically Black Colleges and Universities (HBCU) Network of Campus Compact based at Spelman College. With a background in education and anthropology, she has researched processes of socialization and enculturation in African American communities. Her emphasis on the black church has resulted in the presentation of papers and publications on the implications of church experiences for the school performance of African American children.

GARY W. McDONOGH is a professor of sociology and director of the Program in Growth and Structure of Cities at Bryn Mawr College. Author of *Good Families of Barcelona* and *Black and Catholic in Savannah, Georgia,* he is editor of *The Florida Negro: A Federal Writer's Project Legacy* and *Conflict in Catalonia.* He researches urban power and its representations, the production and reception of literary and visual culture, and comparative urban form and society.

BEATRIZ MORALES, who teaches anthropology at Georgia State University, has also taught at Hunter College, Tulane University, and the University of New Orleans. Her major research areas include ethnicity, urban anthropology, and religion, especially among post-colonial populations. Her work on Latino religion, ritual, and culture is scheduled for publication in the *Handbook of Hispanic Cultures in the United States—Anthropology.*

SHARLOTTE NEELY is a professor of anthropology and coordinator of anthropology at Northern Kentucky University. The author of *Snowbird Cherokees*

(Georgia, 1990), she is currently engaged in research with the Shawnee Nation United Remnant Band.

GWEN KENNEDY NEVILLE is the Elizabeth Root Paden Professor of Anthropology at Southwestern University. She is the author of *Kinship and Pilgrimage* and, with Miles Richardson, was among the founding members of the Southern Anthropological Society.

MONA TAYLOR PHILLIPS received her doctorate in sociology from the University of Michigan at Ann Arbor and is an associate professor at Spelman College. Her areas of research, writing, and teaching are African American women, institutional and cultural racism and sexism, and black women's health.

MILES RICHARDSON is the Fred B. Kniffen Professor of Geography and Anthropology at Louisiana State University. Both a southerner and an anthropologist who works in Spanish America, Richardson discovers in the contrasting images of Christ in the South and Spanish America strategies to put death in its place, strategies that, because we are flesh-and-blood creatures, inevitably fail. He also marvels at the incompatibility of his two identities as a southerner and an anthropologist in *Cry Lonesome and Other Accounts of the Anthropologist's Project*.

KARY D. SMOUT is an assistant professor of English, director of the Writing Center, and coordinator of the Writing Program at Washington and Lee University. His research and teaching interests include language, rhetoric, and American literature.

BRENDA G. STEWART is a graduate student at the University of North Carolina at Chapel Hill, working on a doctorate in anthropology.

SCOTT LEE THUMMA is a doctoral candidate in the Division of Religion at Emory University. His research interests include the sociology of religion, American religious history, sociology of homosexuality, and social psychology.

MELINDA BOLLAR WAGNER is a professor of anthropology and the associate chair of the Appalachian Studies Program at Radford University in Radford, Virginia. She has conducted research on both New Age and conservative Christian religions and is the author of *Metaphysics in Midwestern America* and *God's Schools: Choice and Compromise in American Society*.

DARYL WHITE is an associate professor of anthropology and chair of the Department of Sociology and Anthropology at Spelman College. He is secretary-treasurer of the Southern Anthropological Society and the author of a number of articles in the anthropology and sociology of religion.

O. KENDALL WHITE JR. is a professor of sociology and chair of the Department of Sociology and Anthropology at Washington and Lee University in Lexington, Virginia. The author of *Mormon Neo-Orthodoxy: A Crisis Theology* and numerous articles on religion, he is completing a book with his brother, Daryl White, on African American Mormons and the Latter Day Saints priesthood.